PICTURE BOOK OF NATURE SCENES

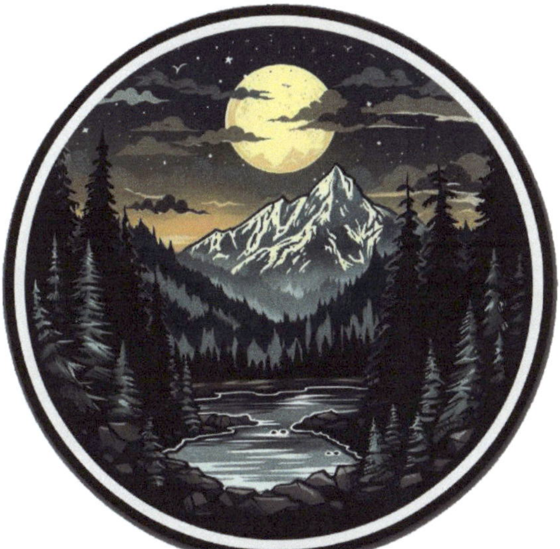

...By...

Ella Caldwell

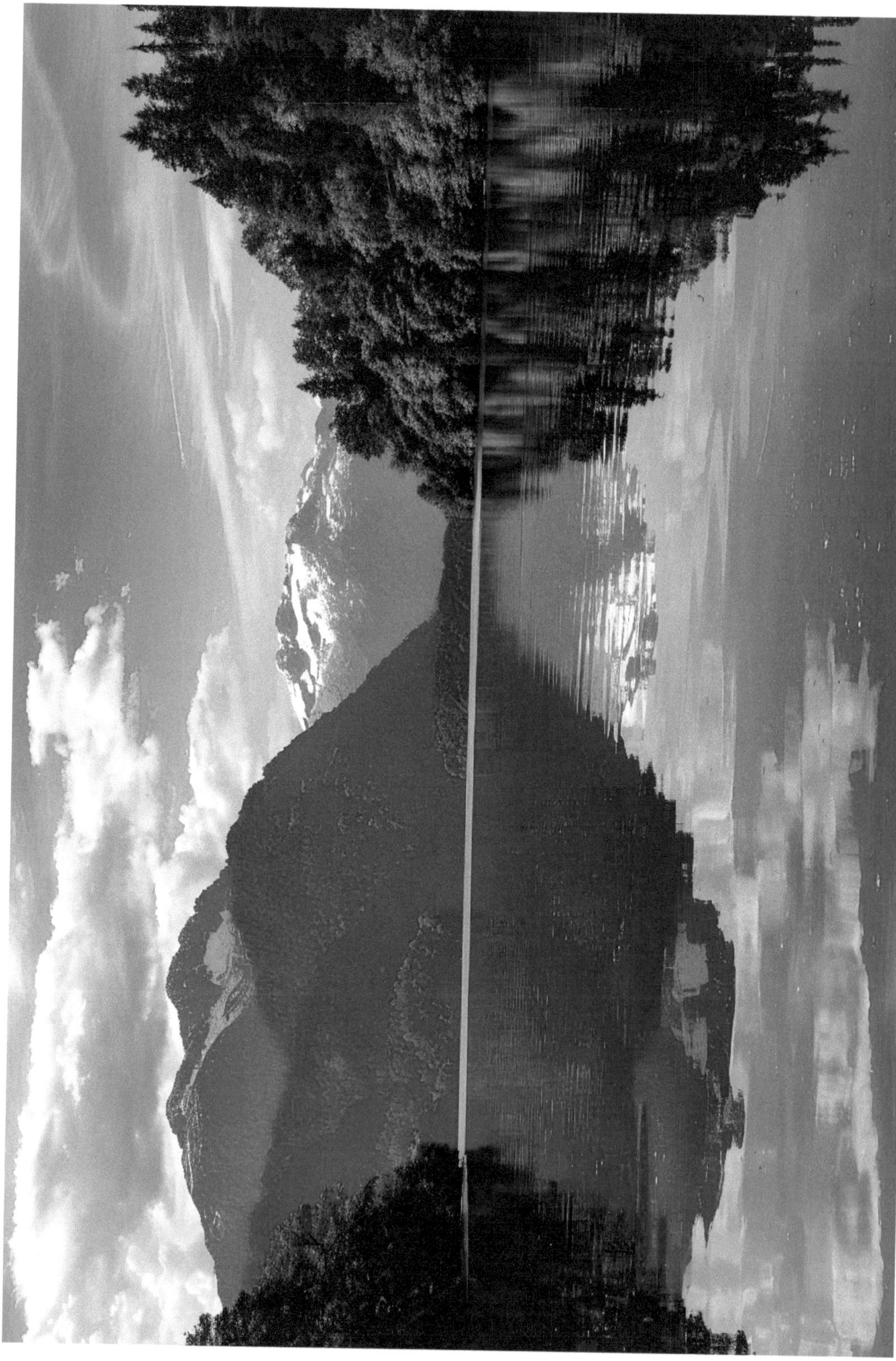

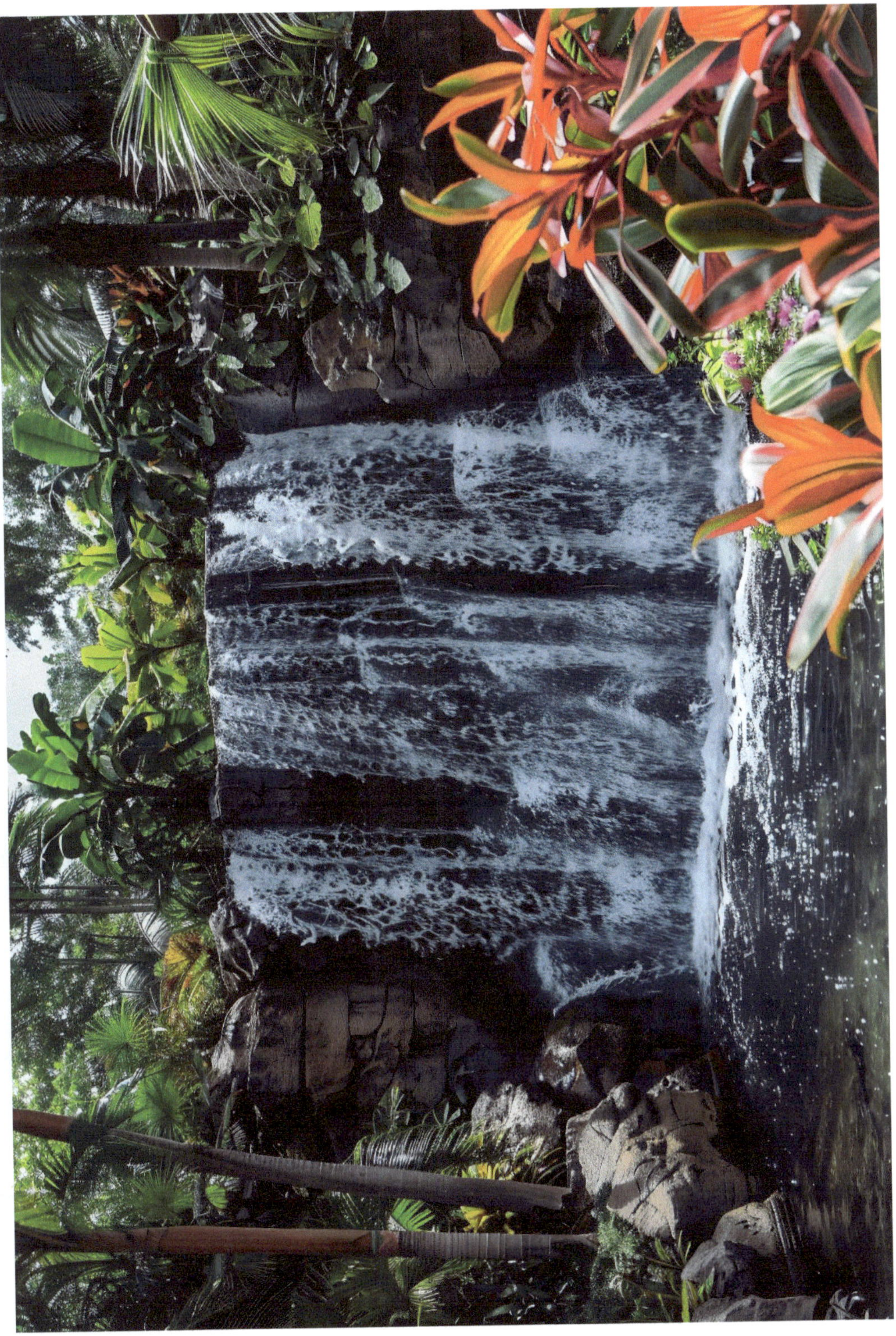

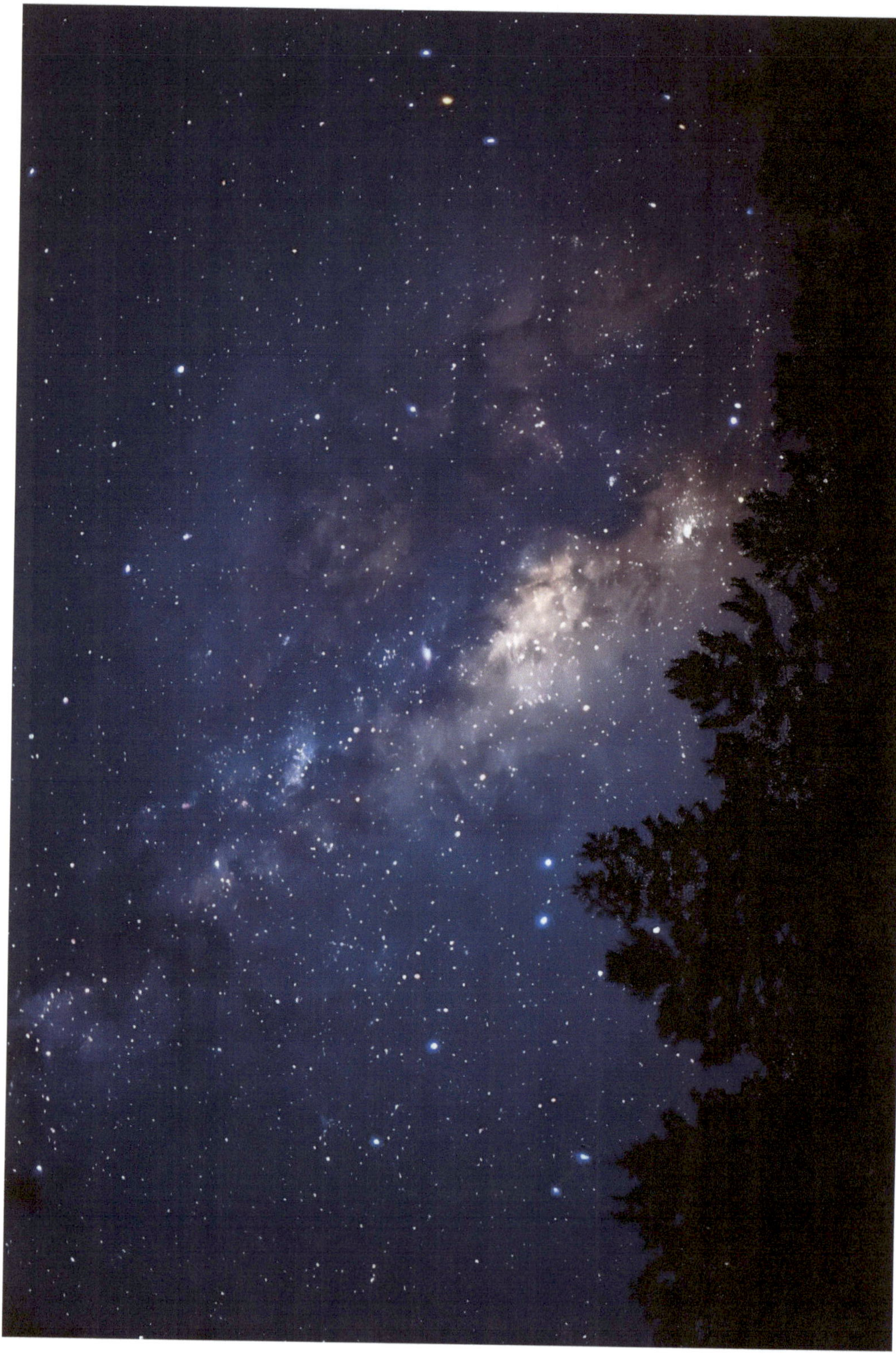

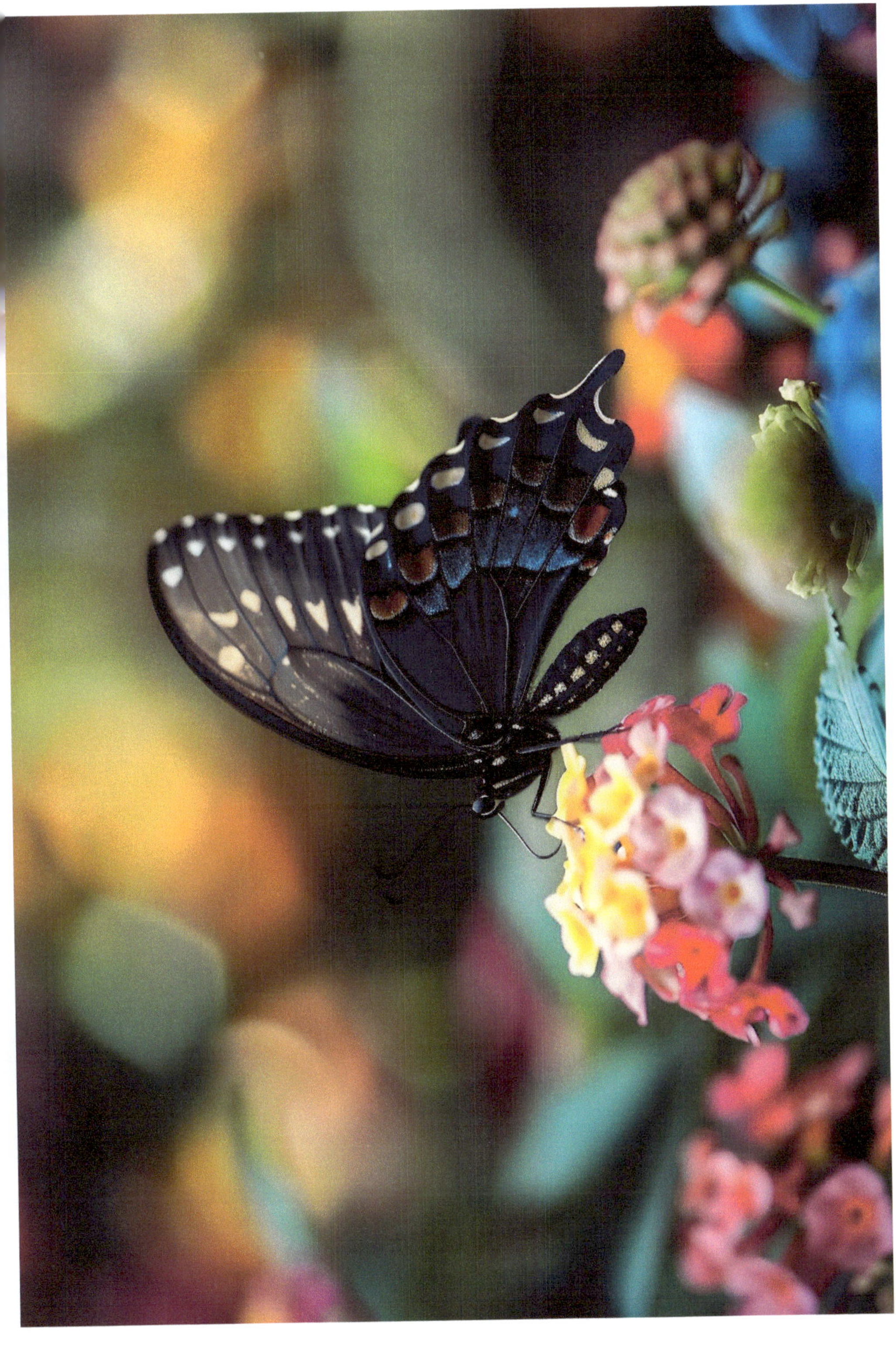

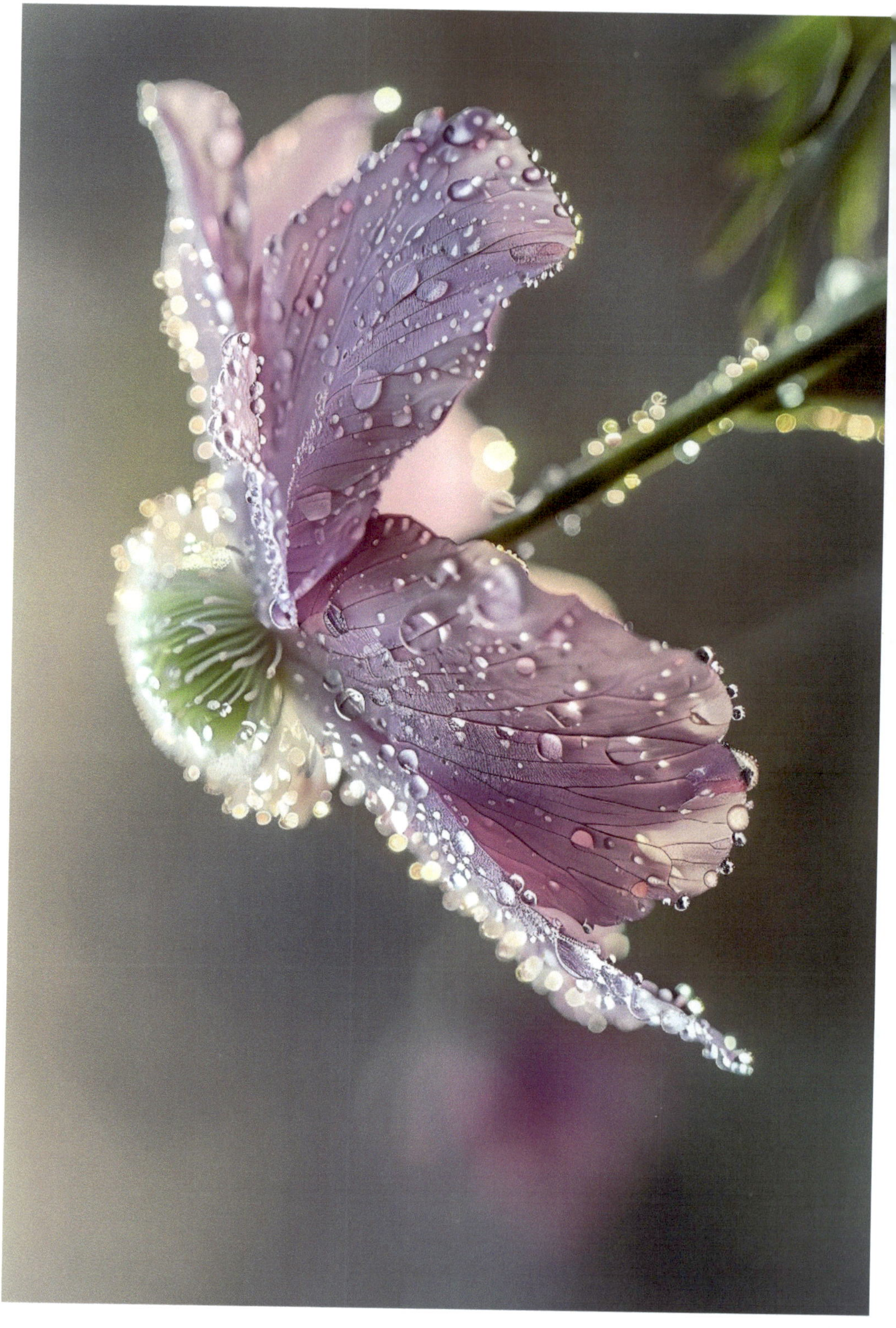

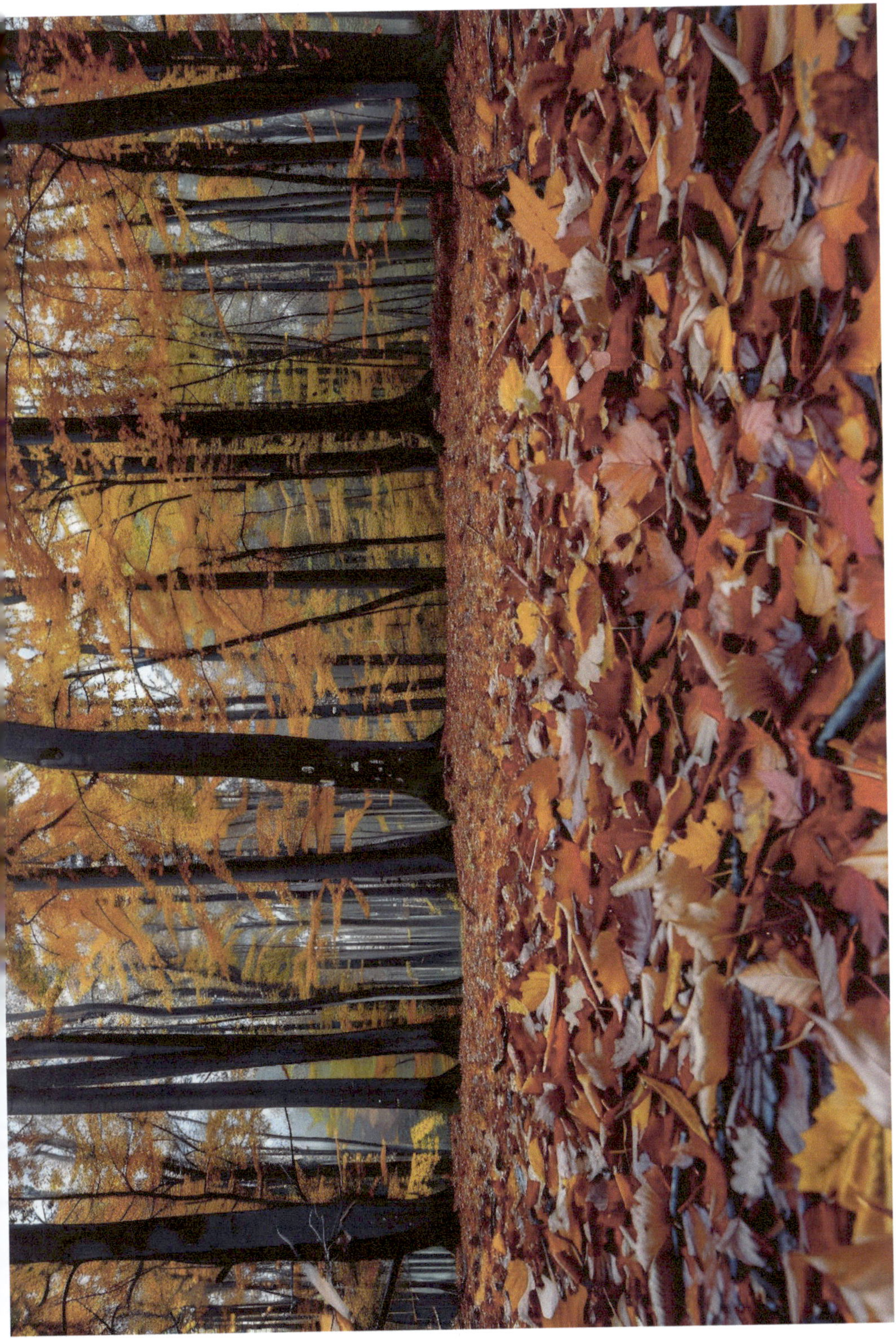

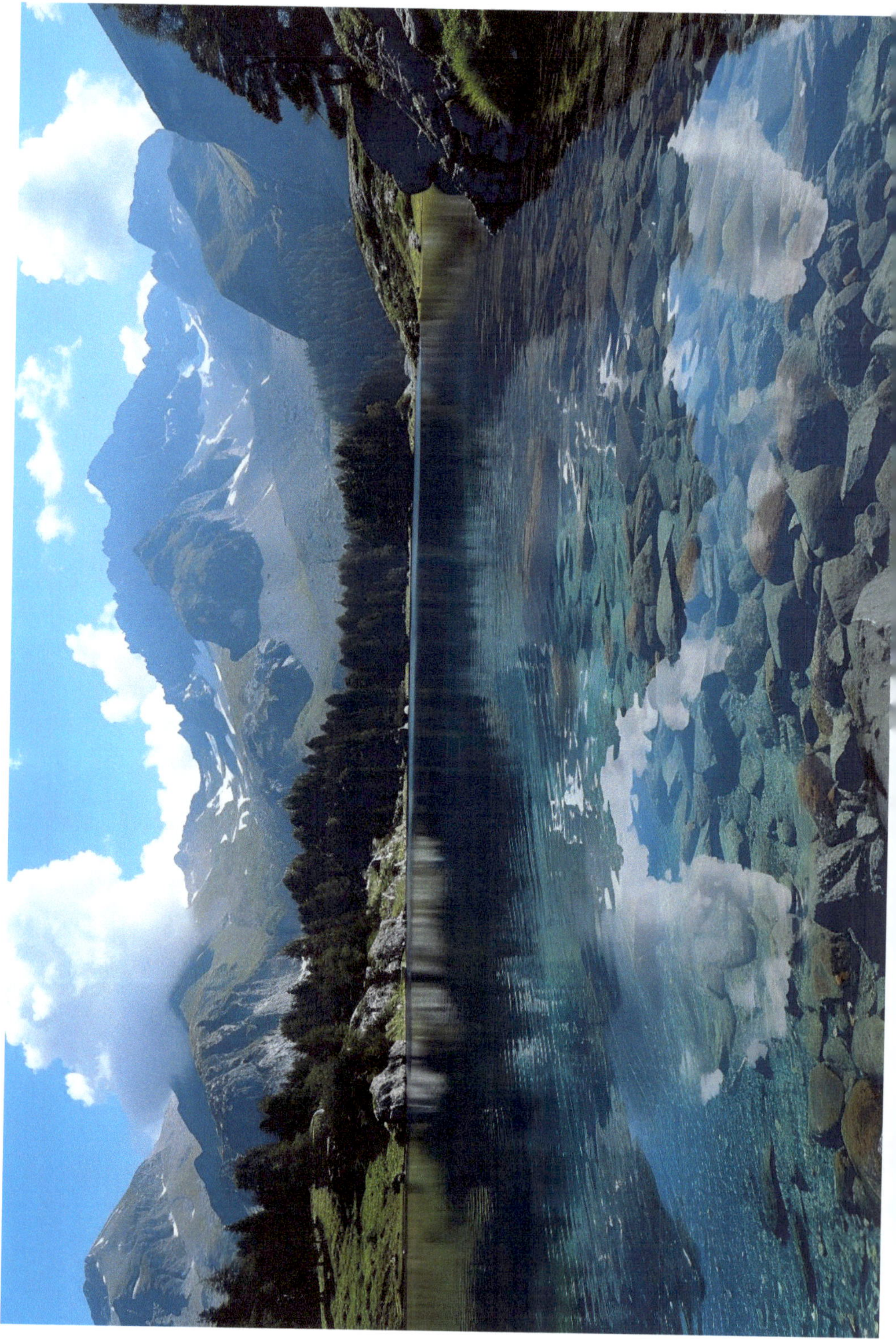

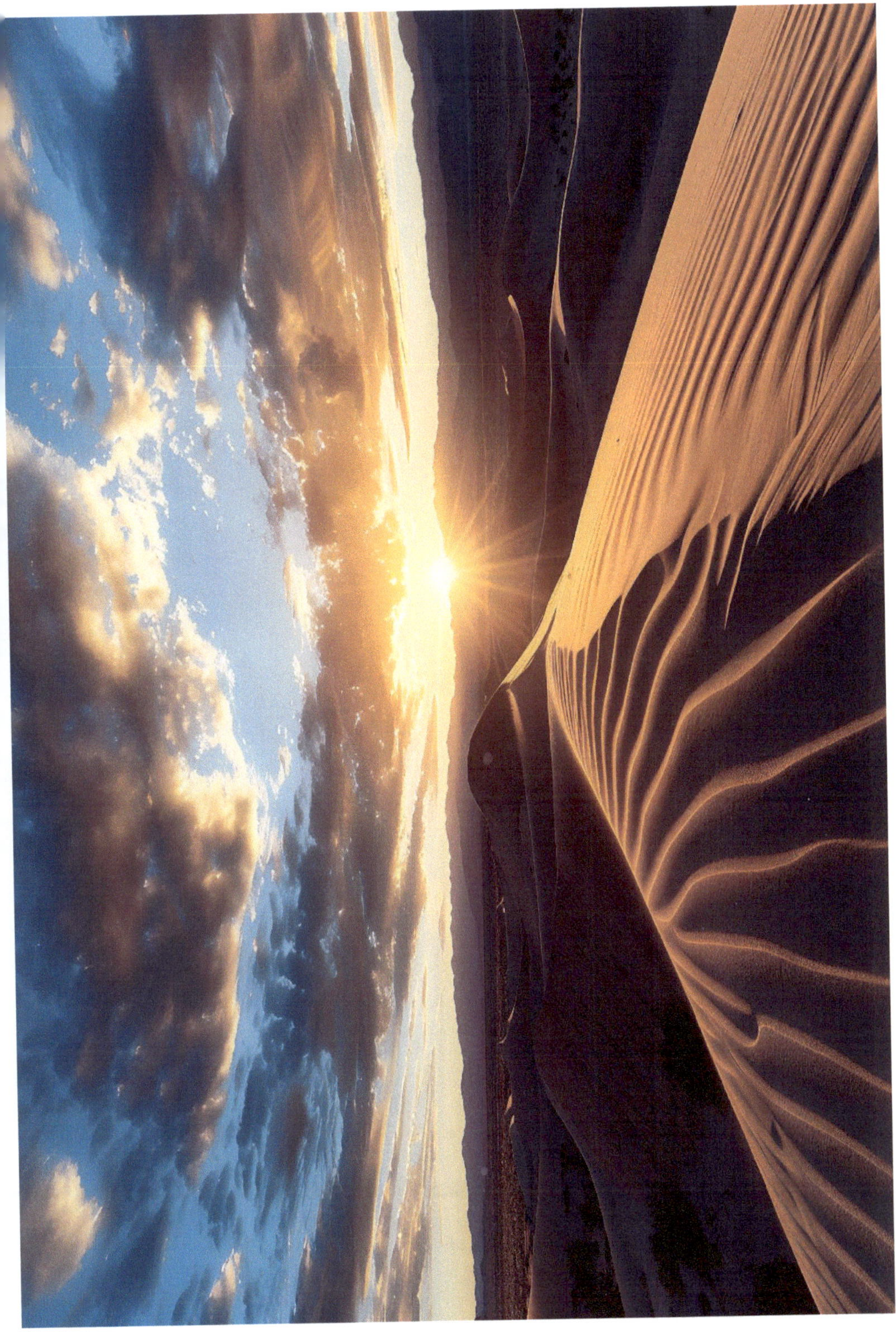

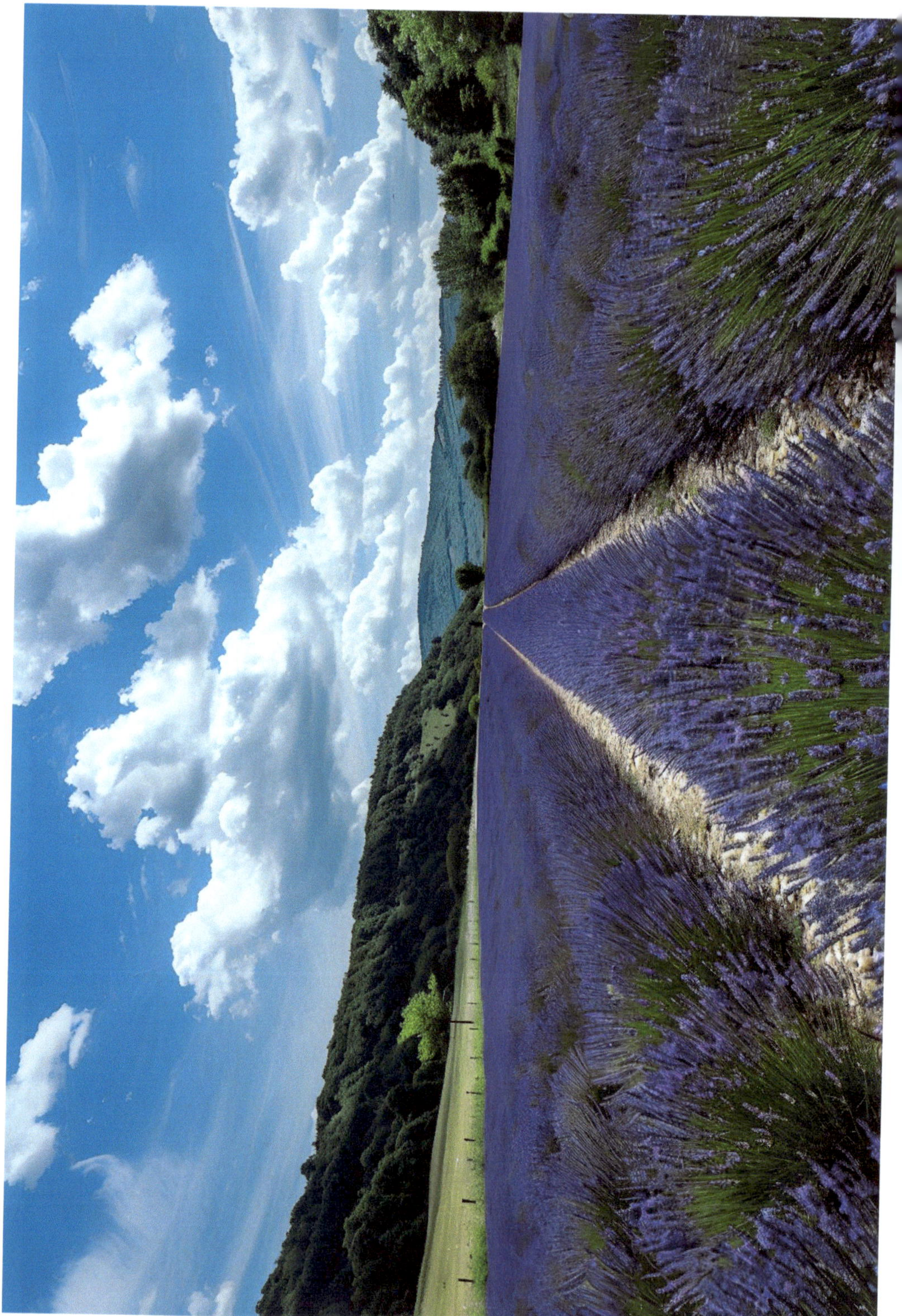

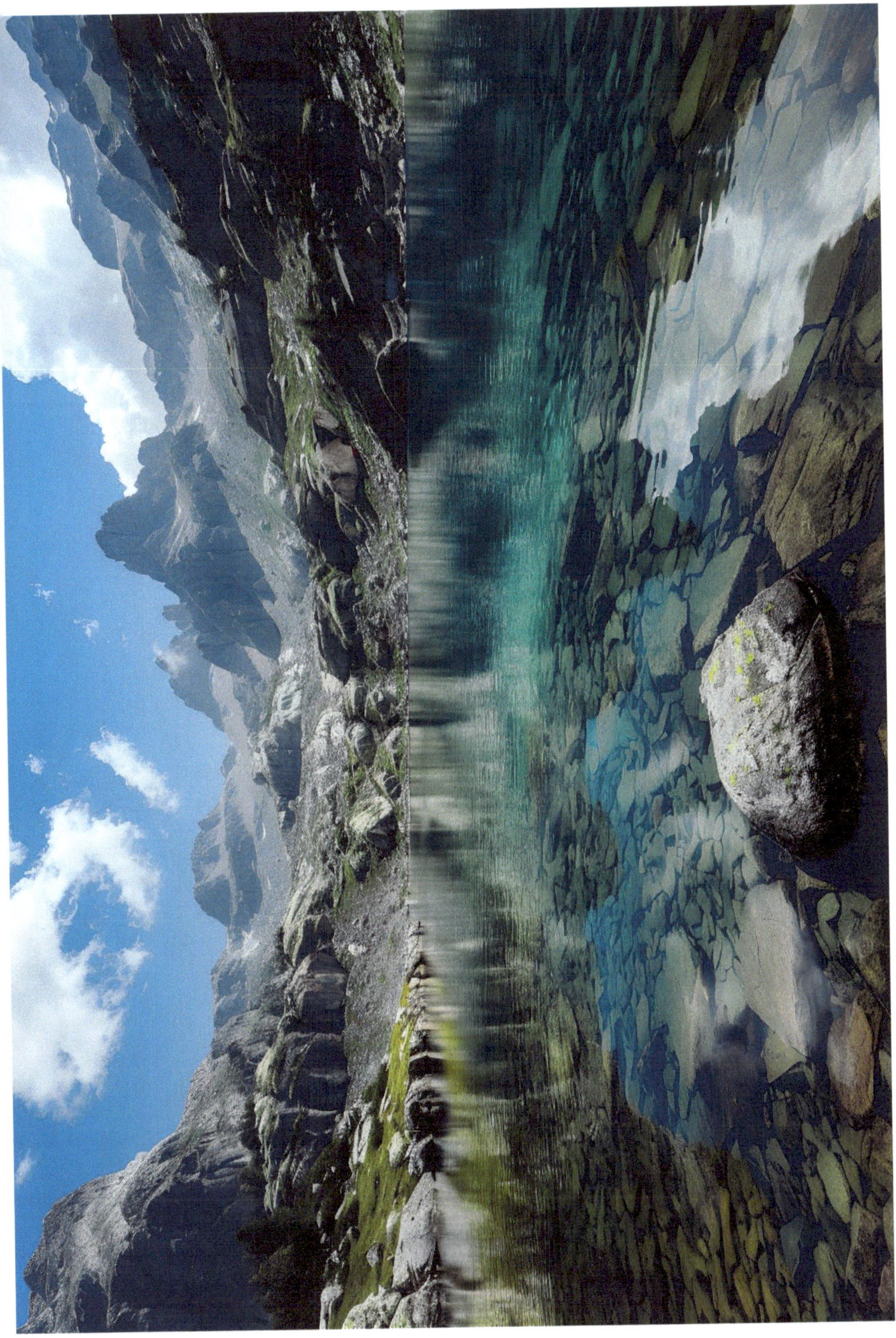

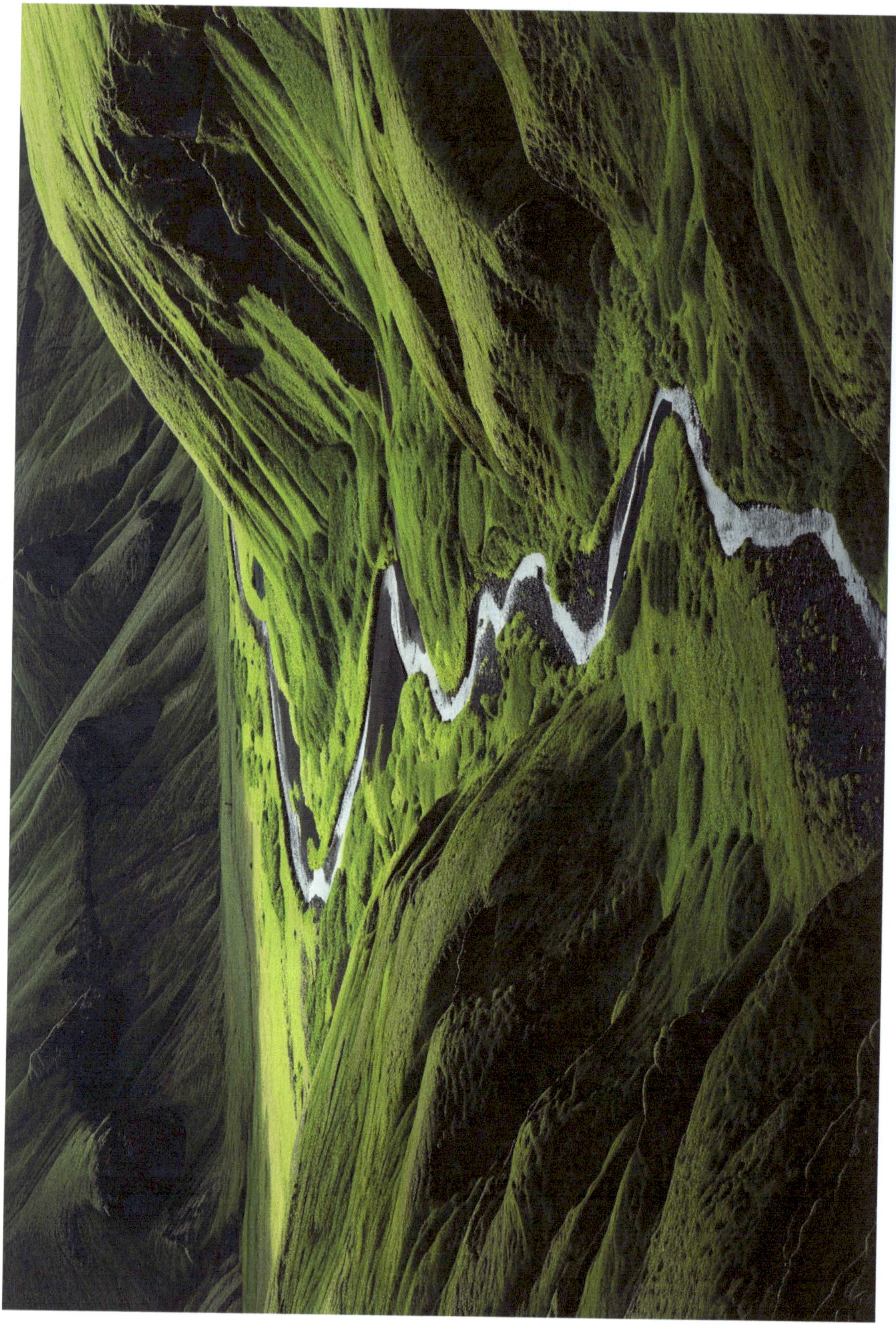

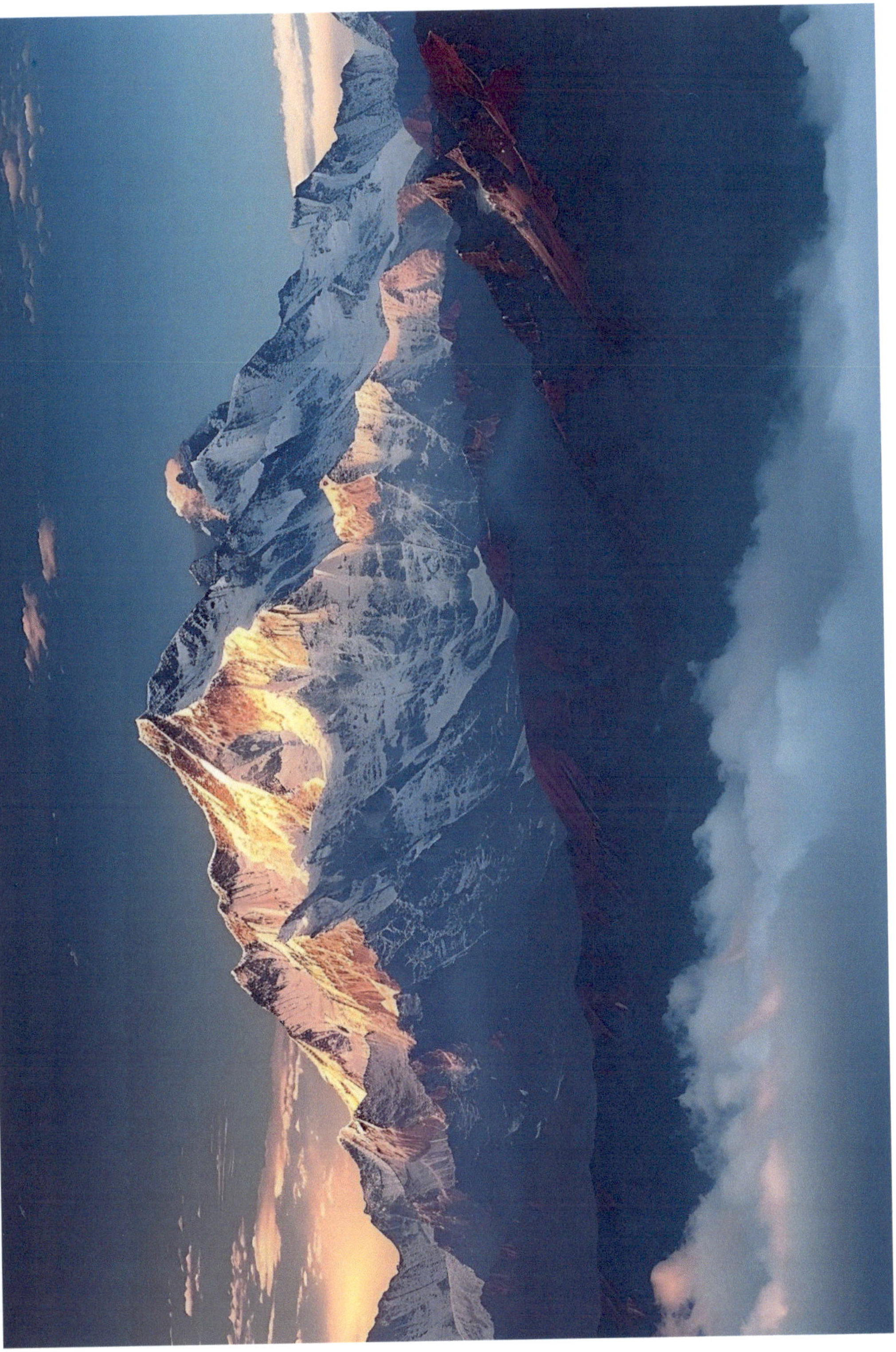

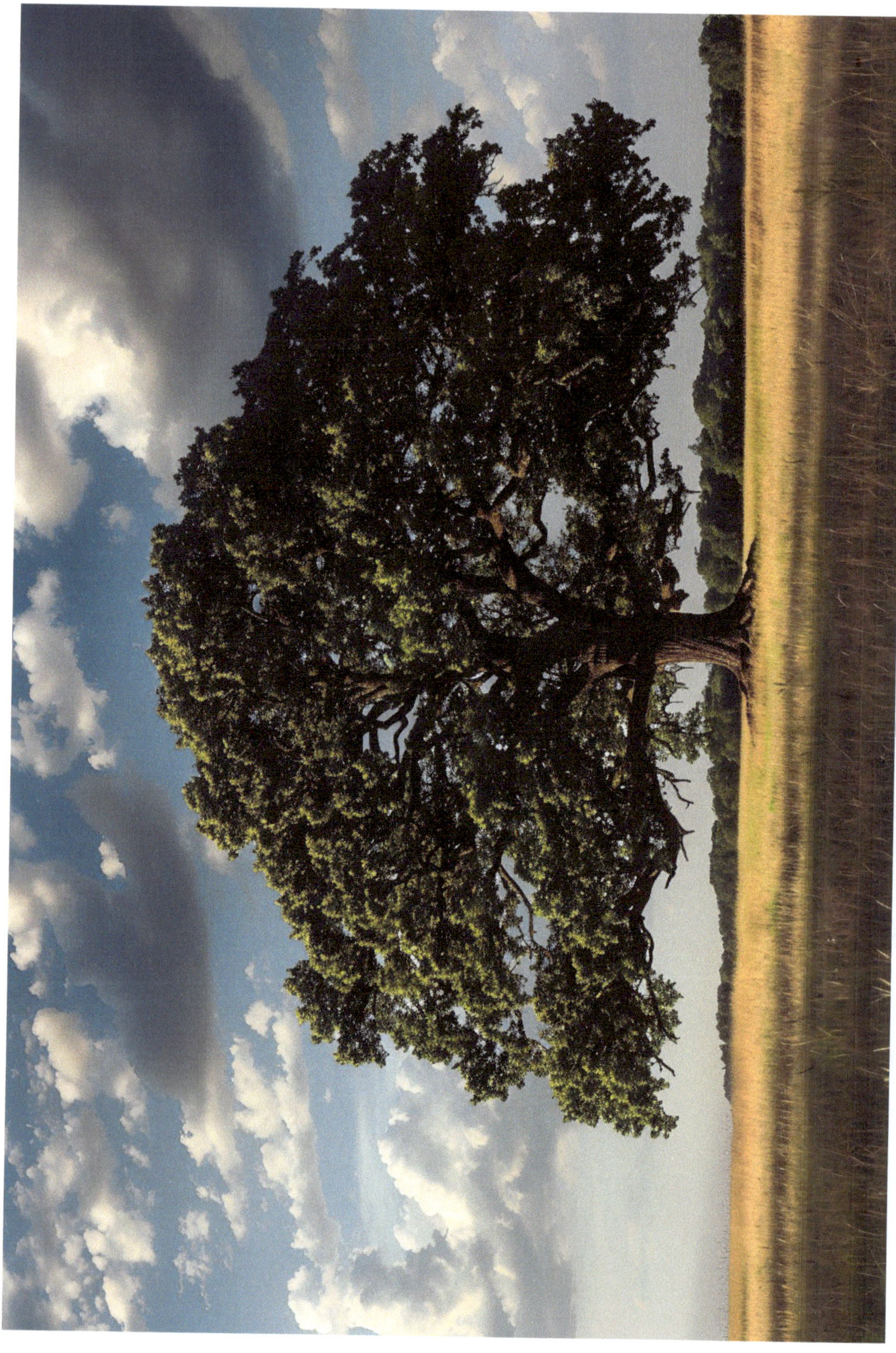

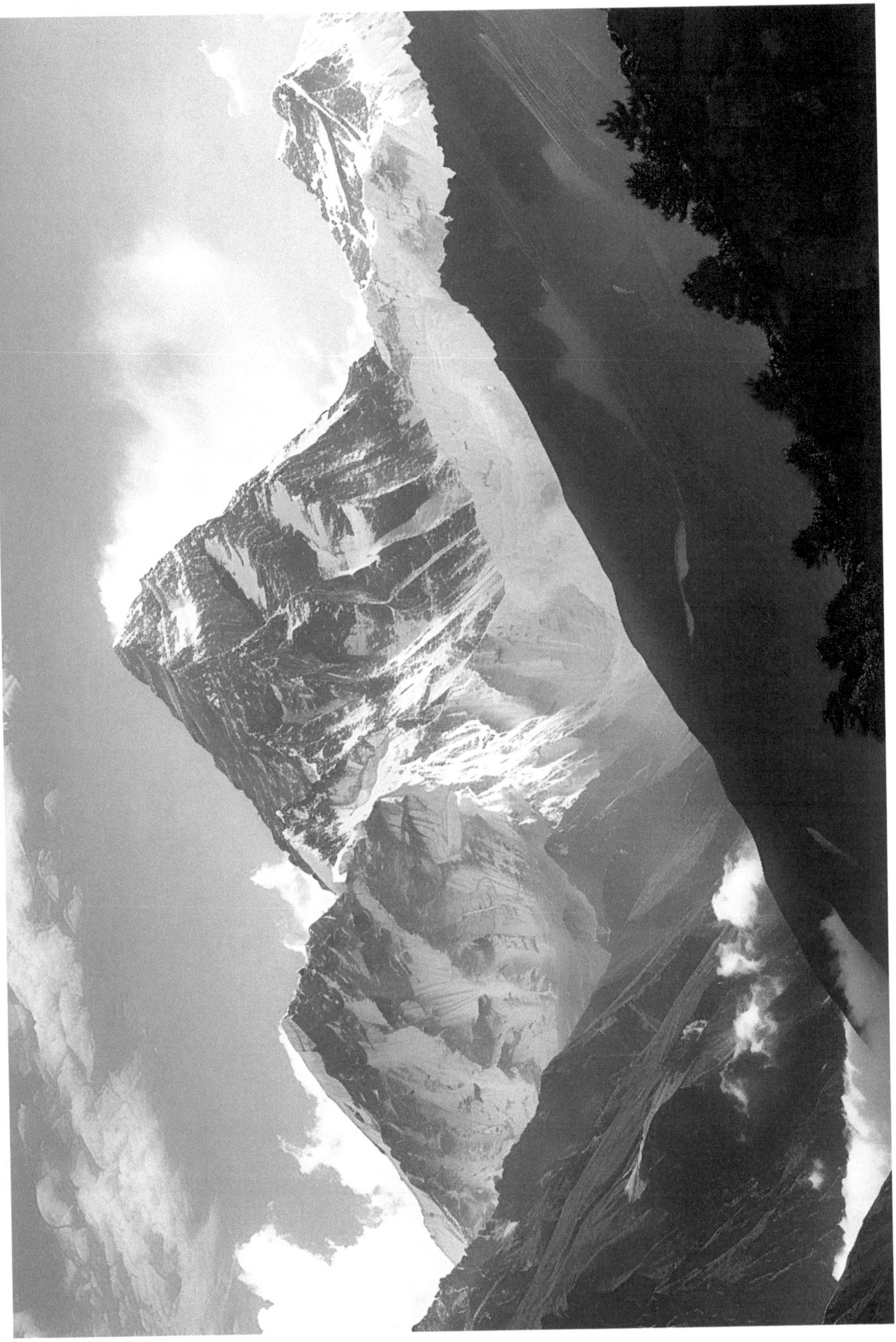

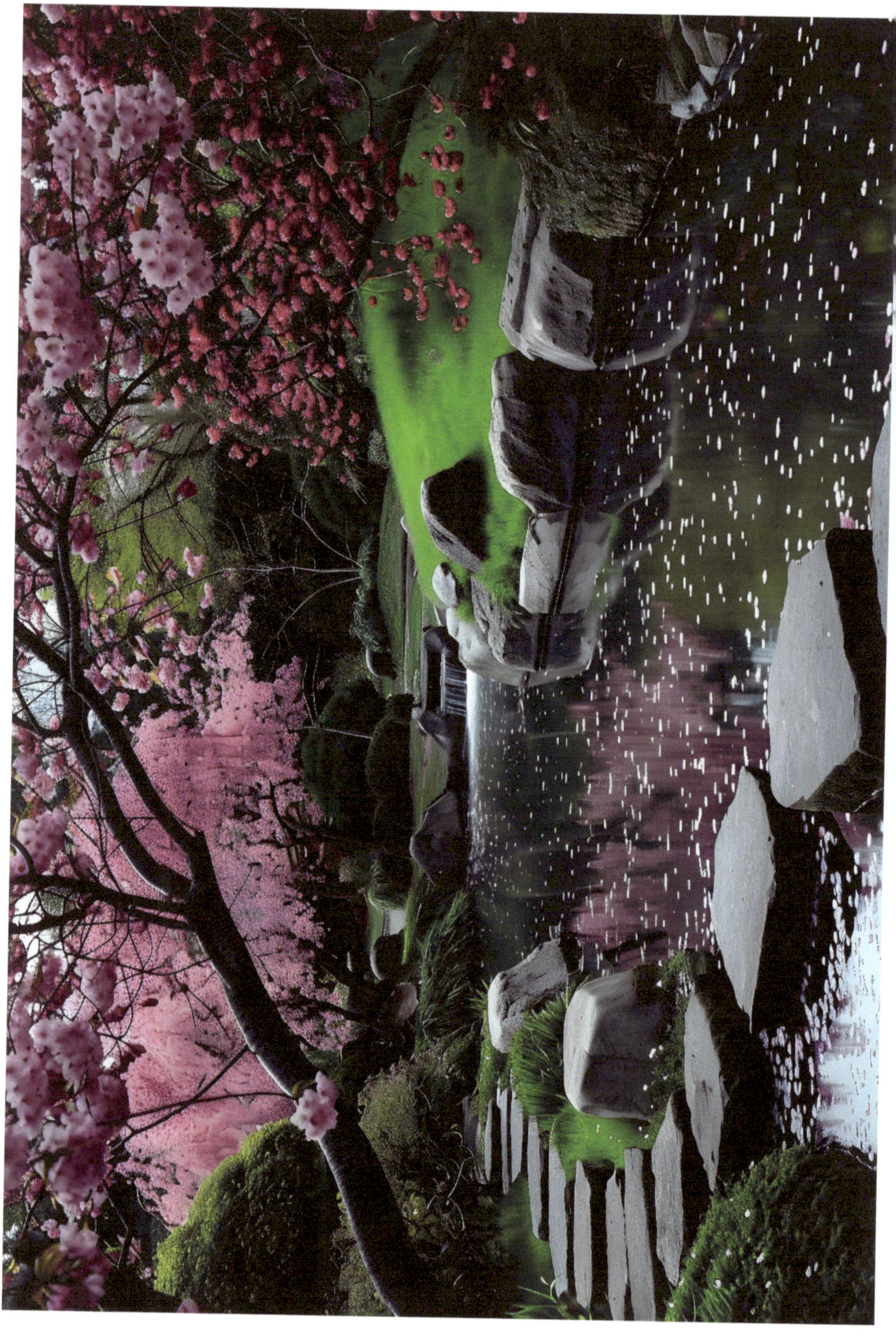

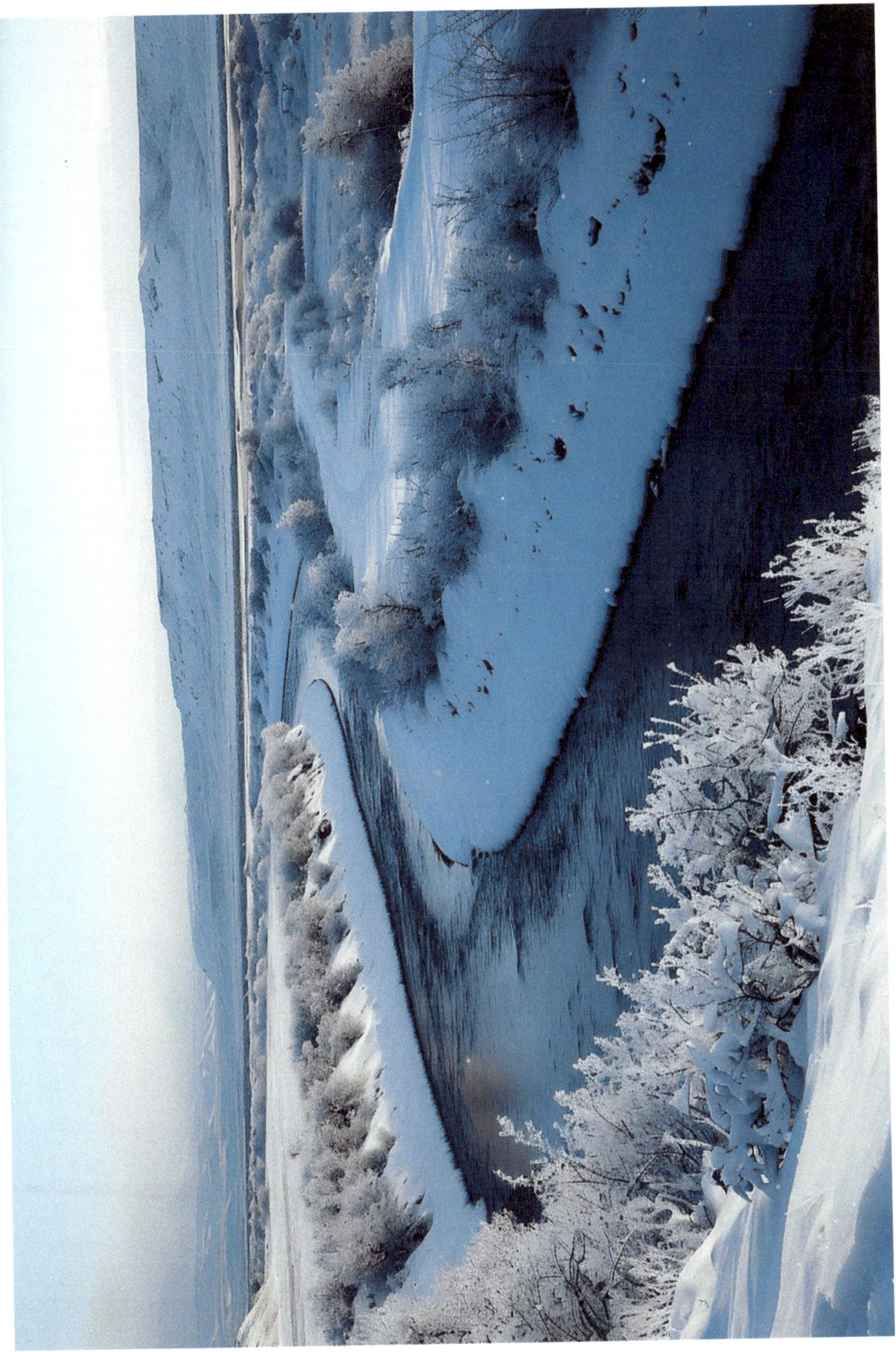

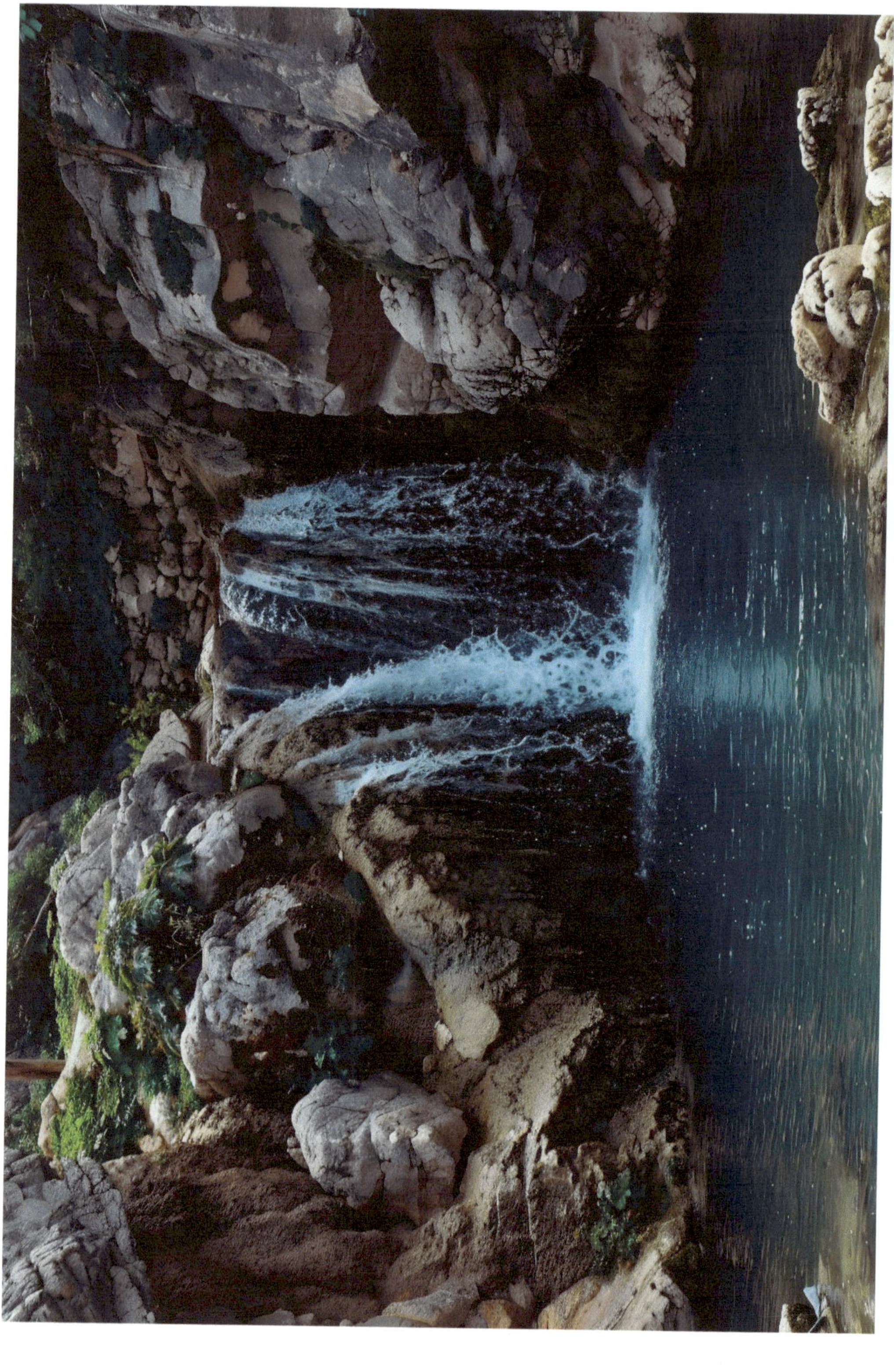

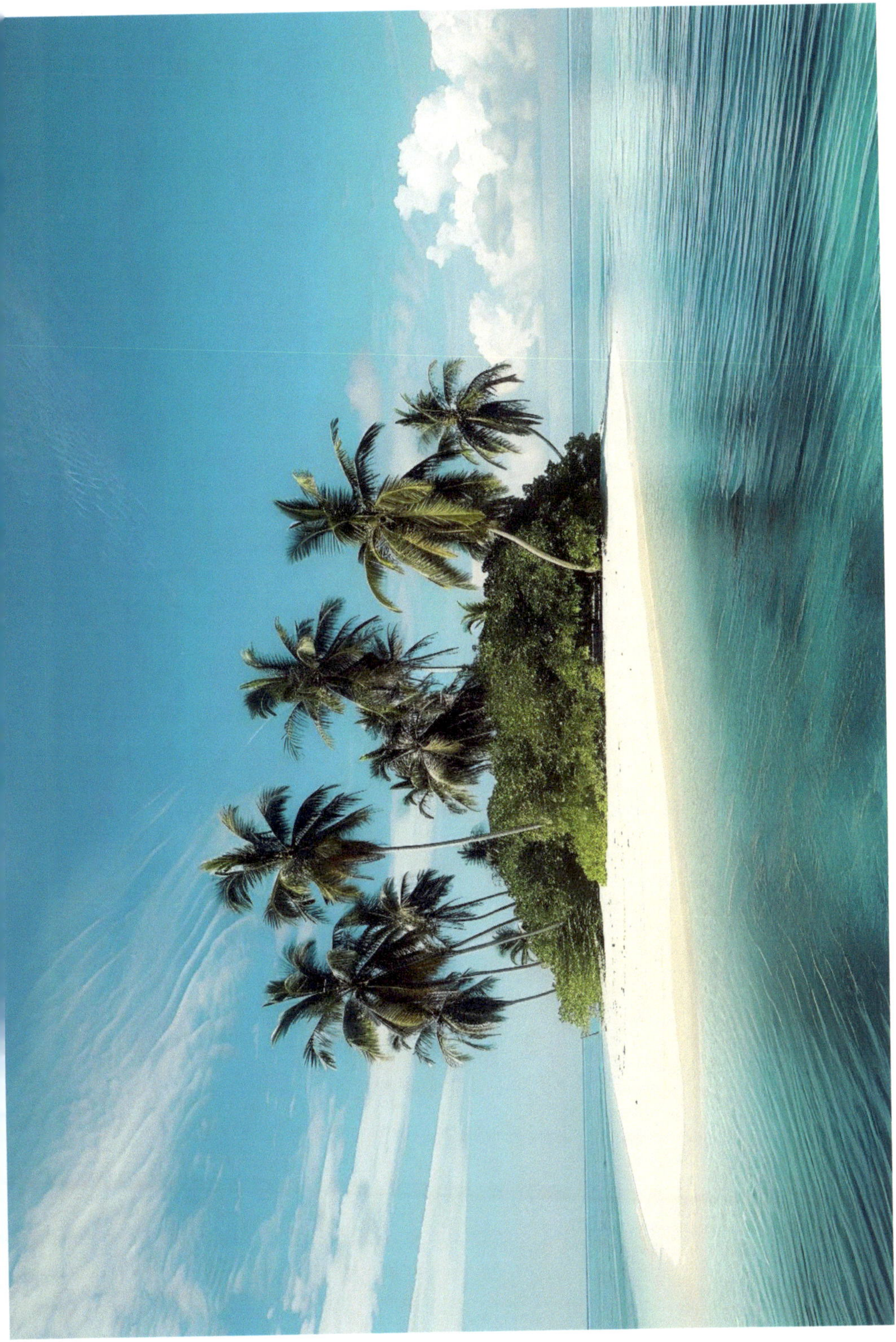

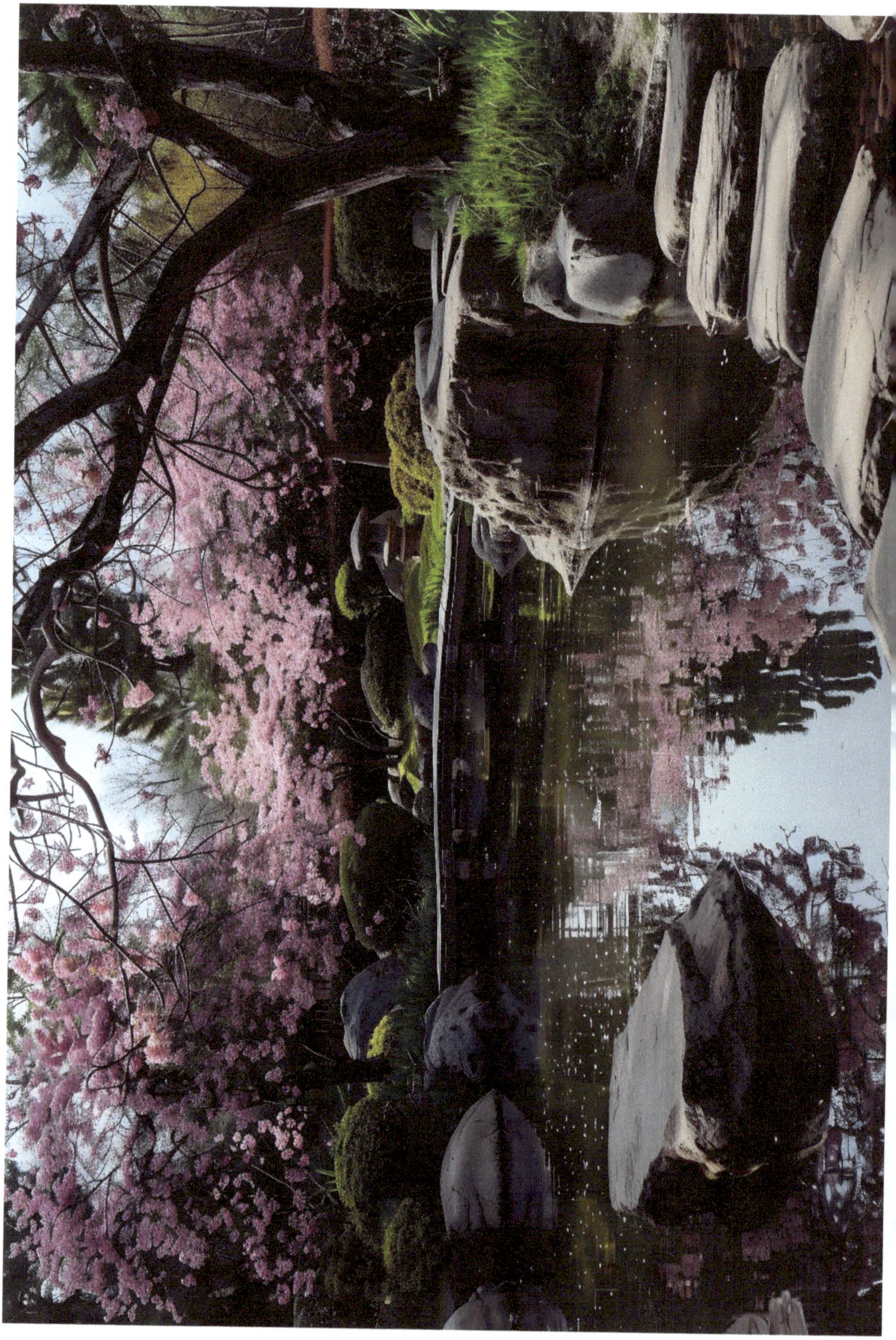

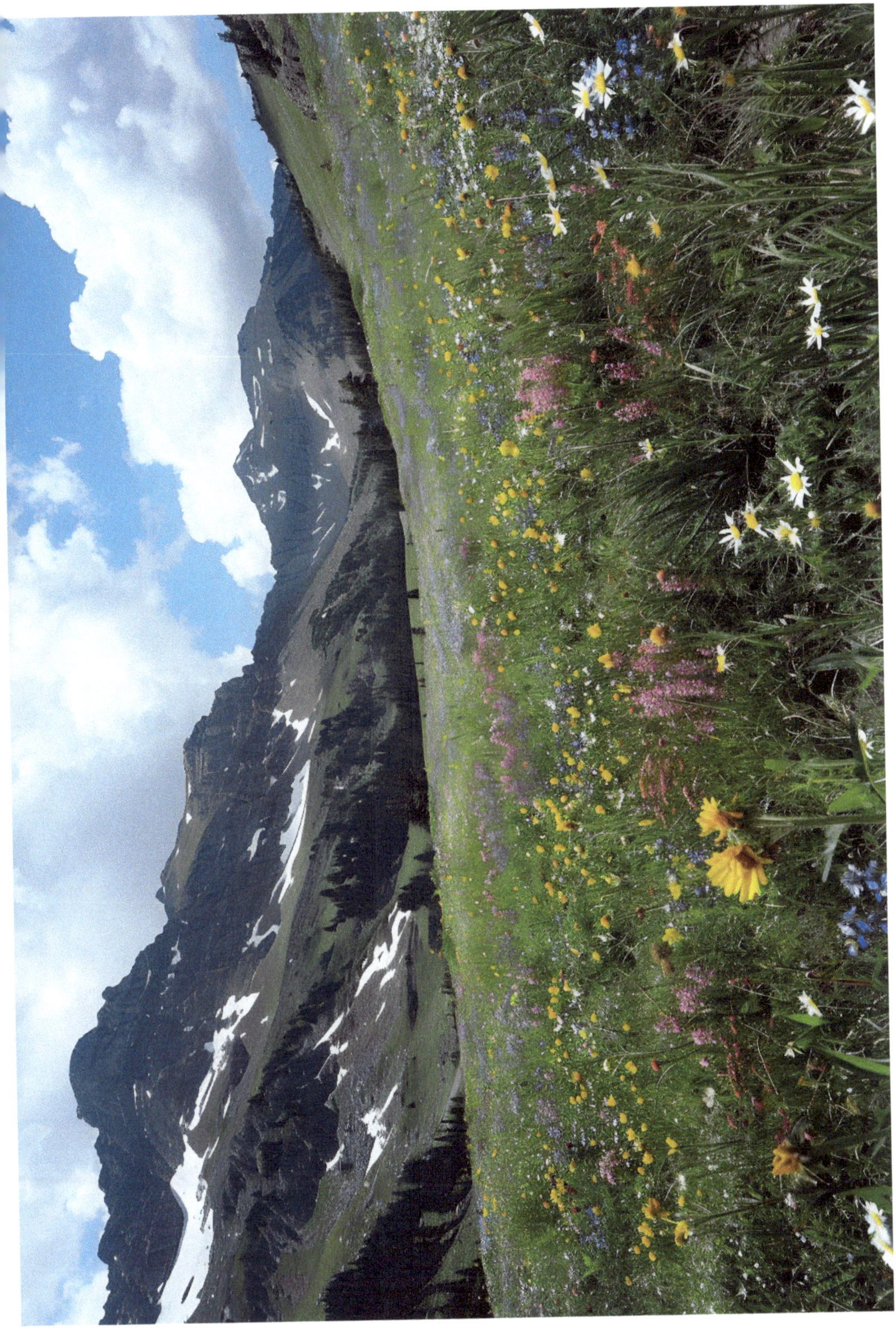

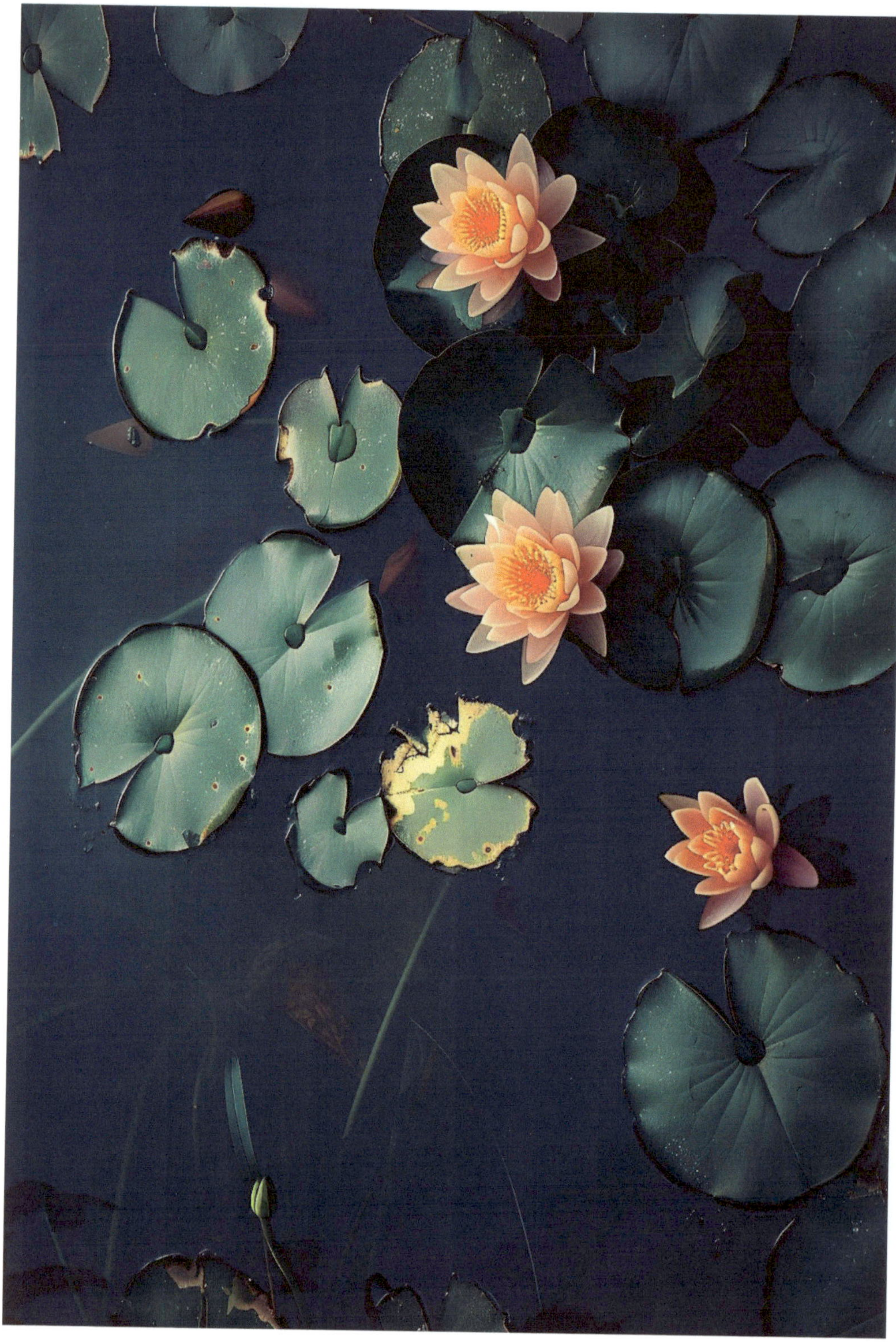

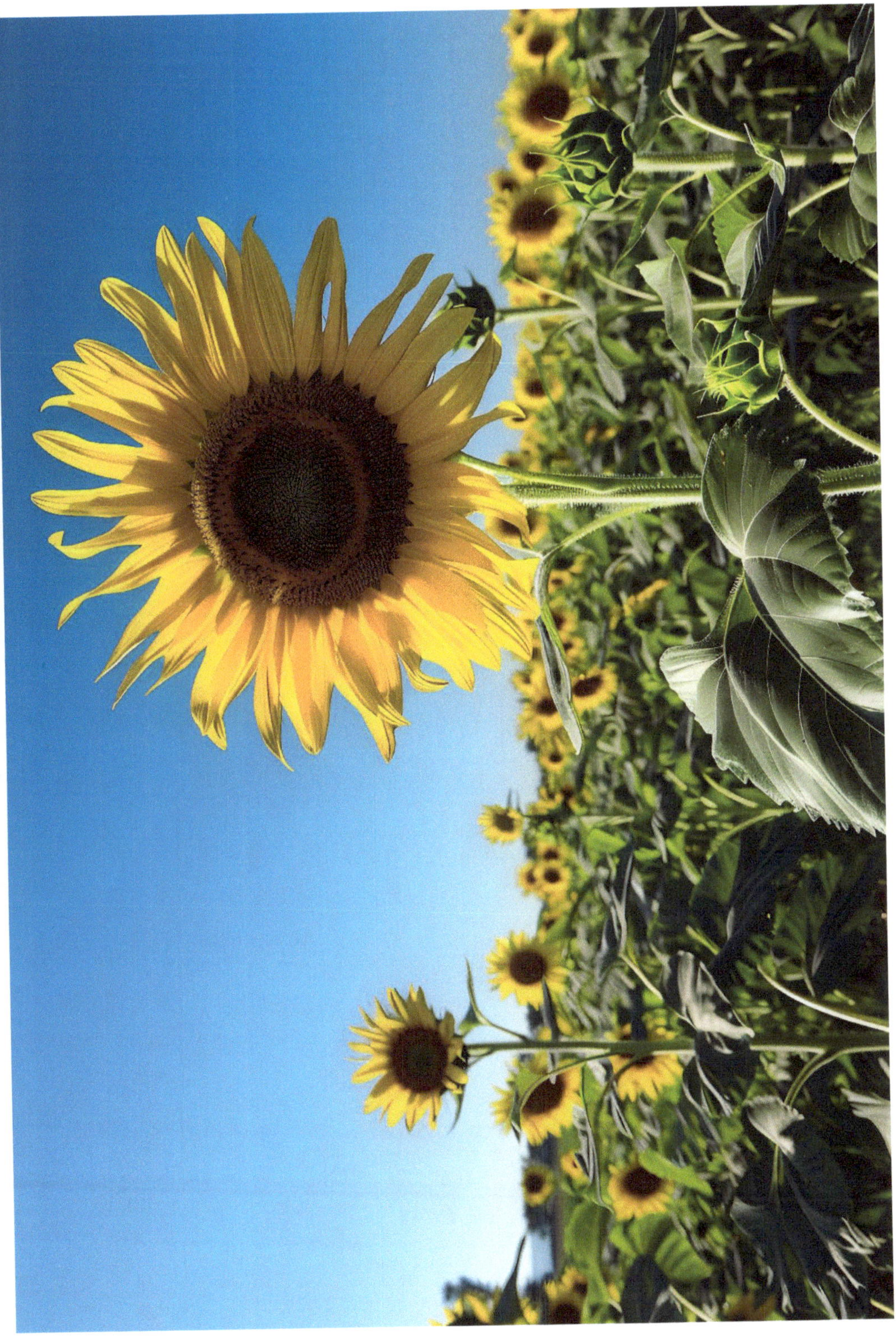

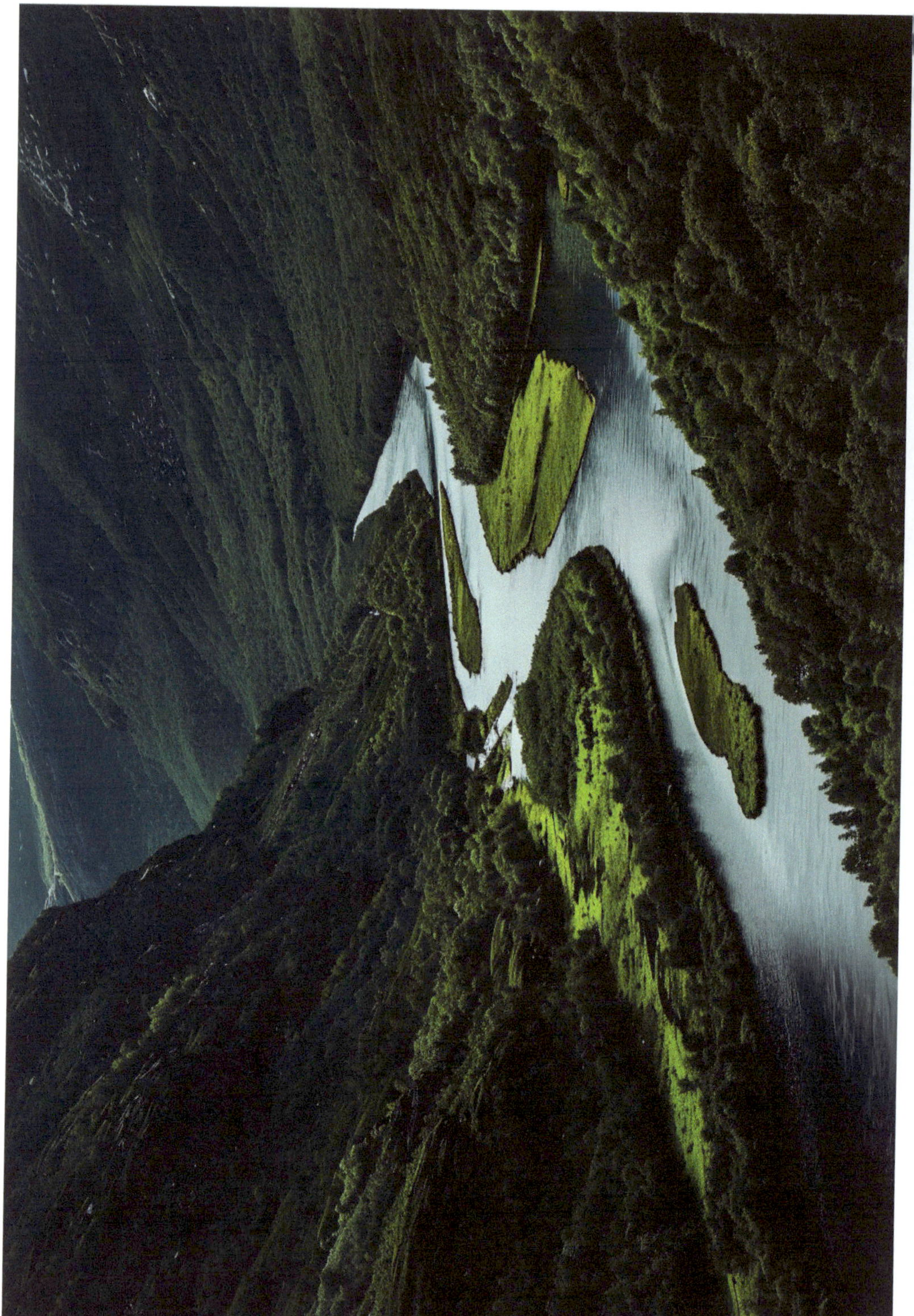

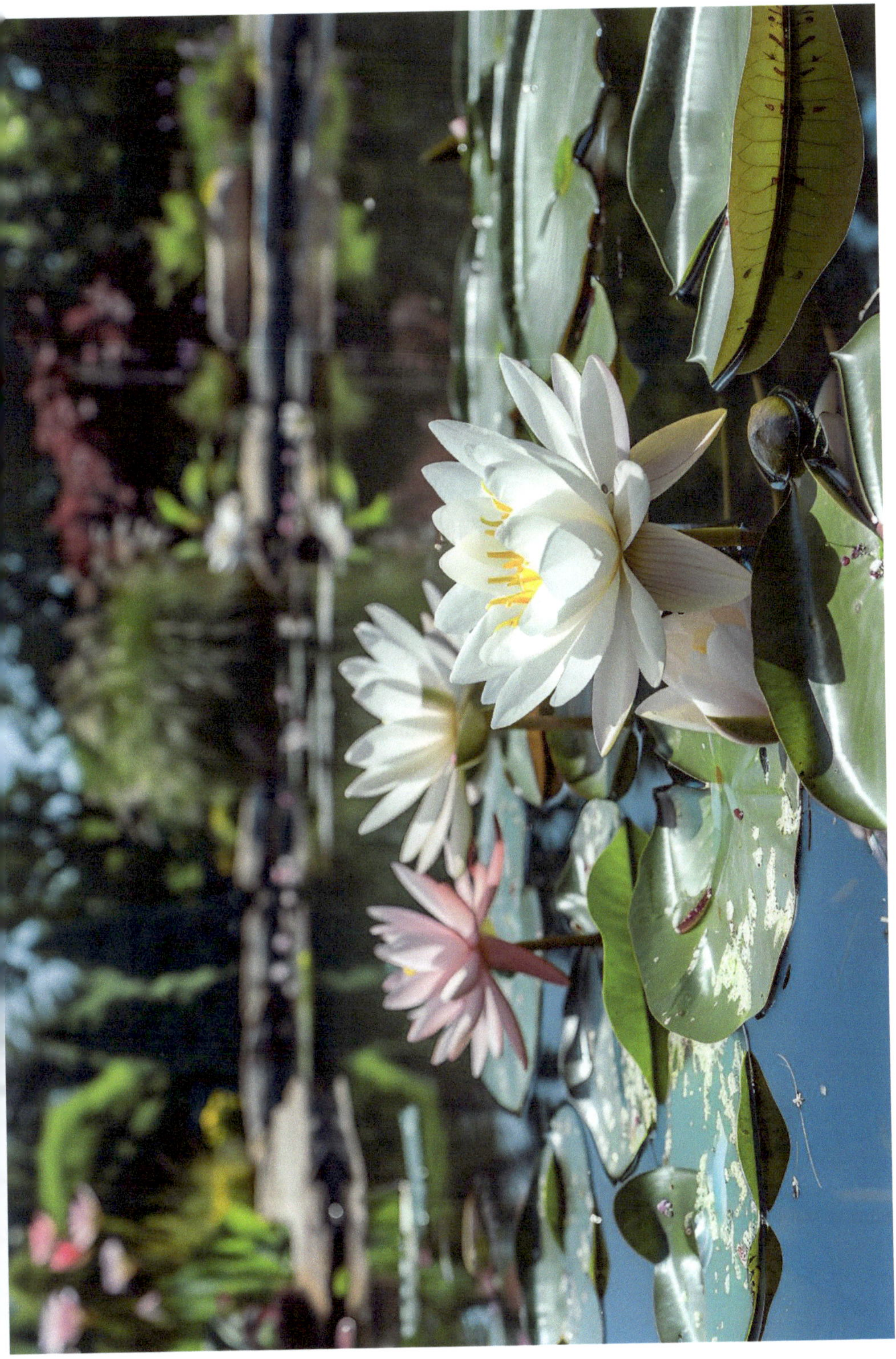

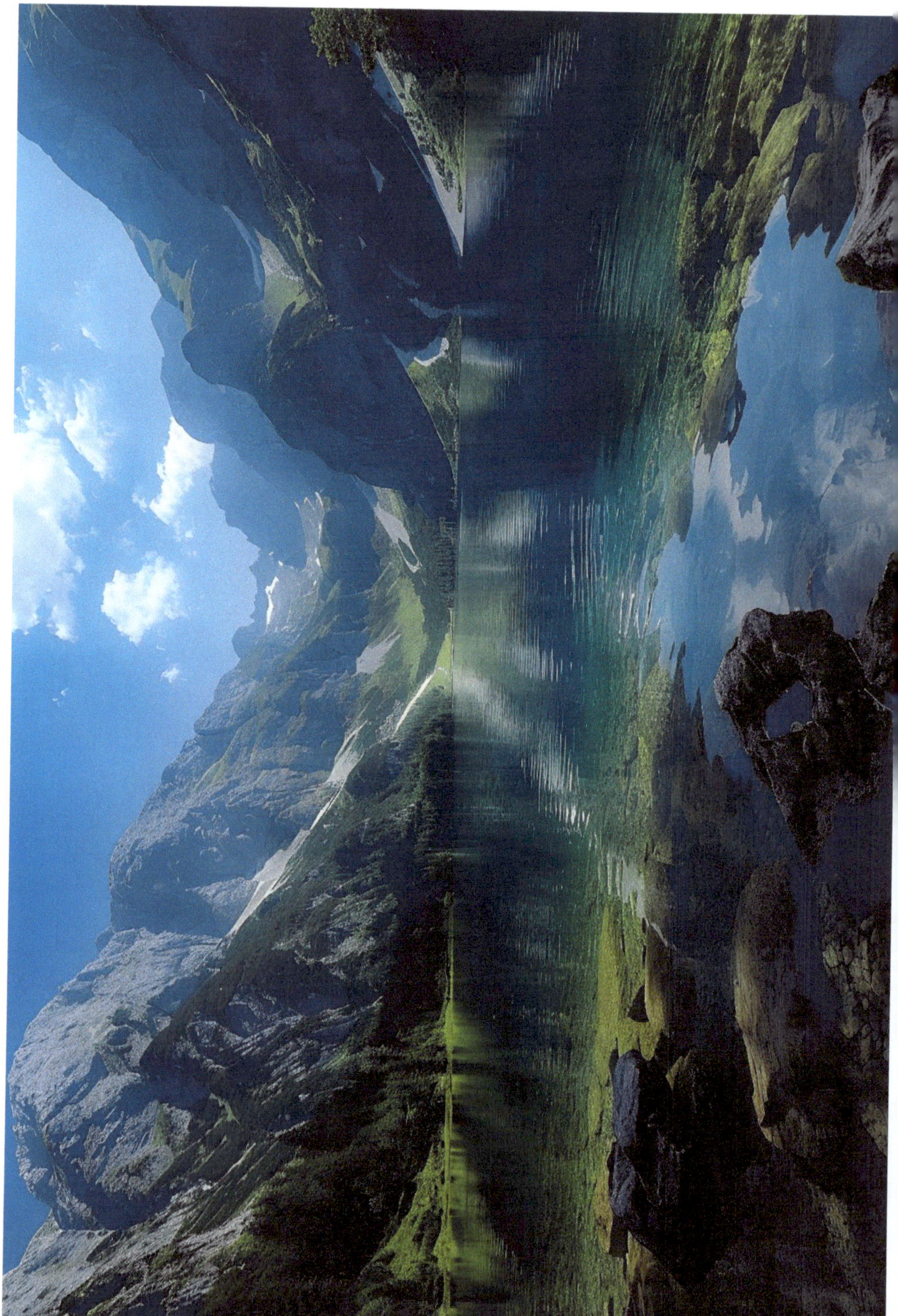

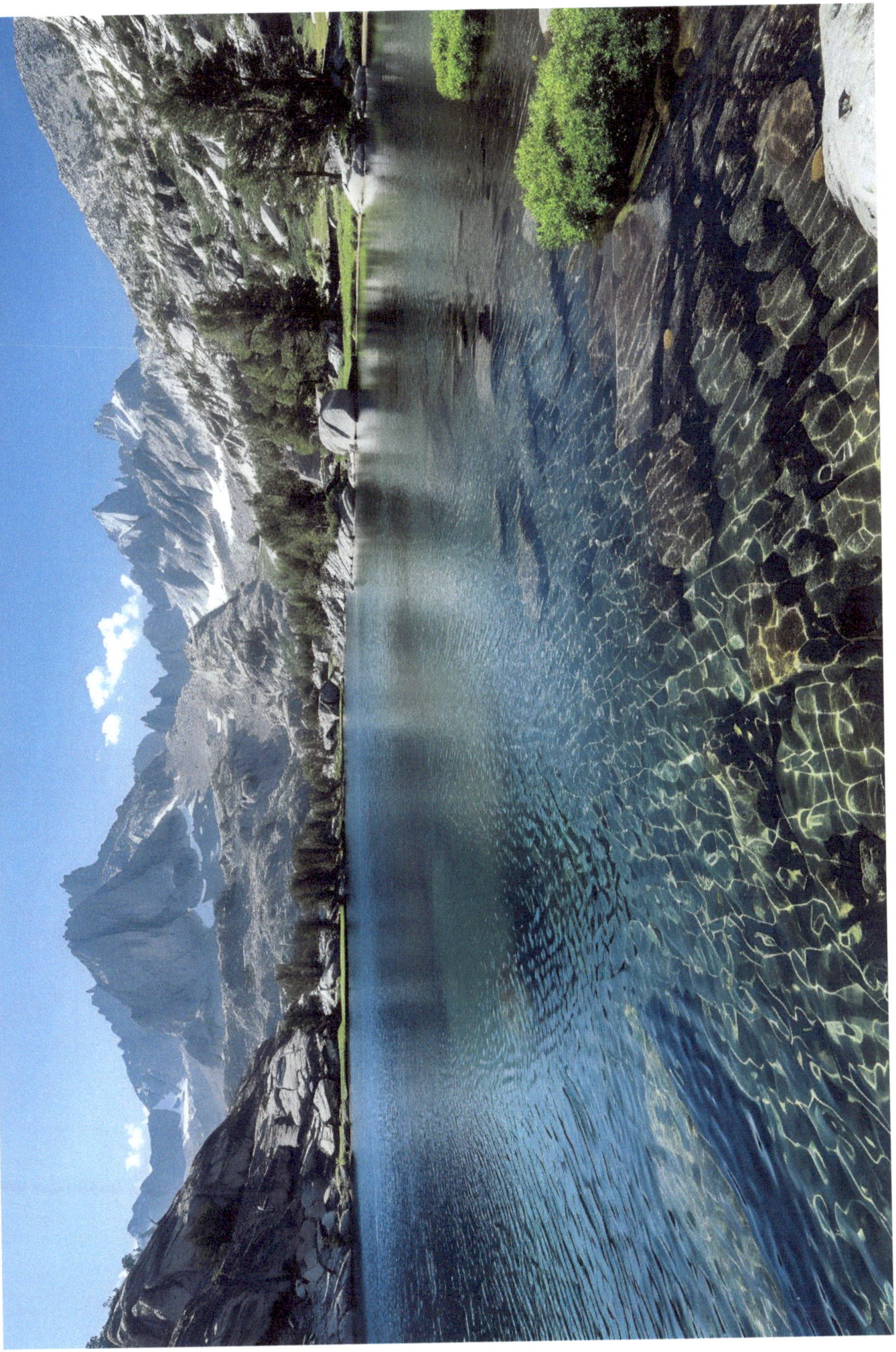

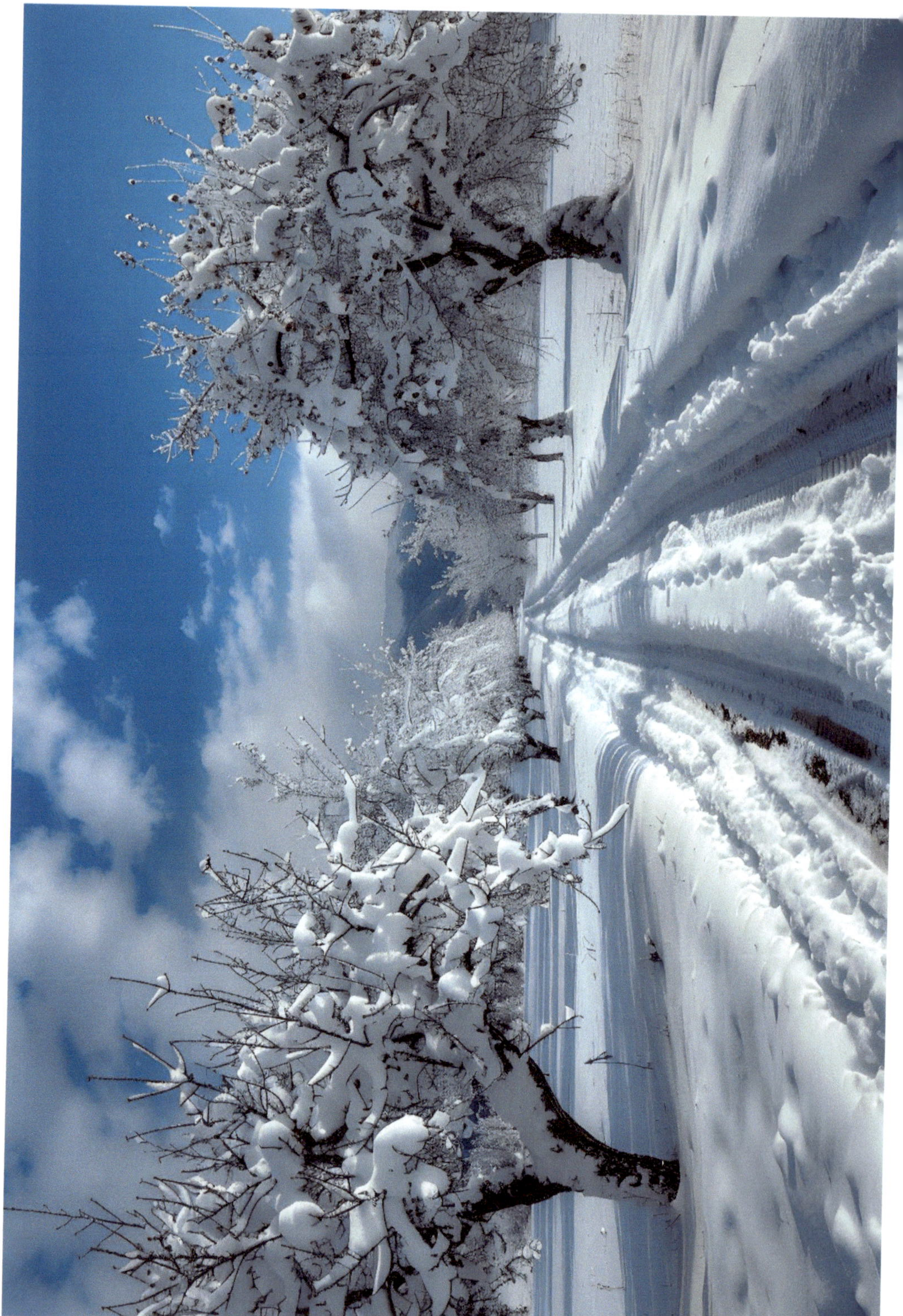

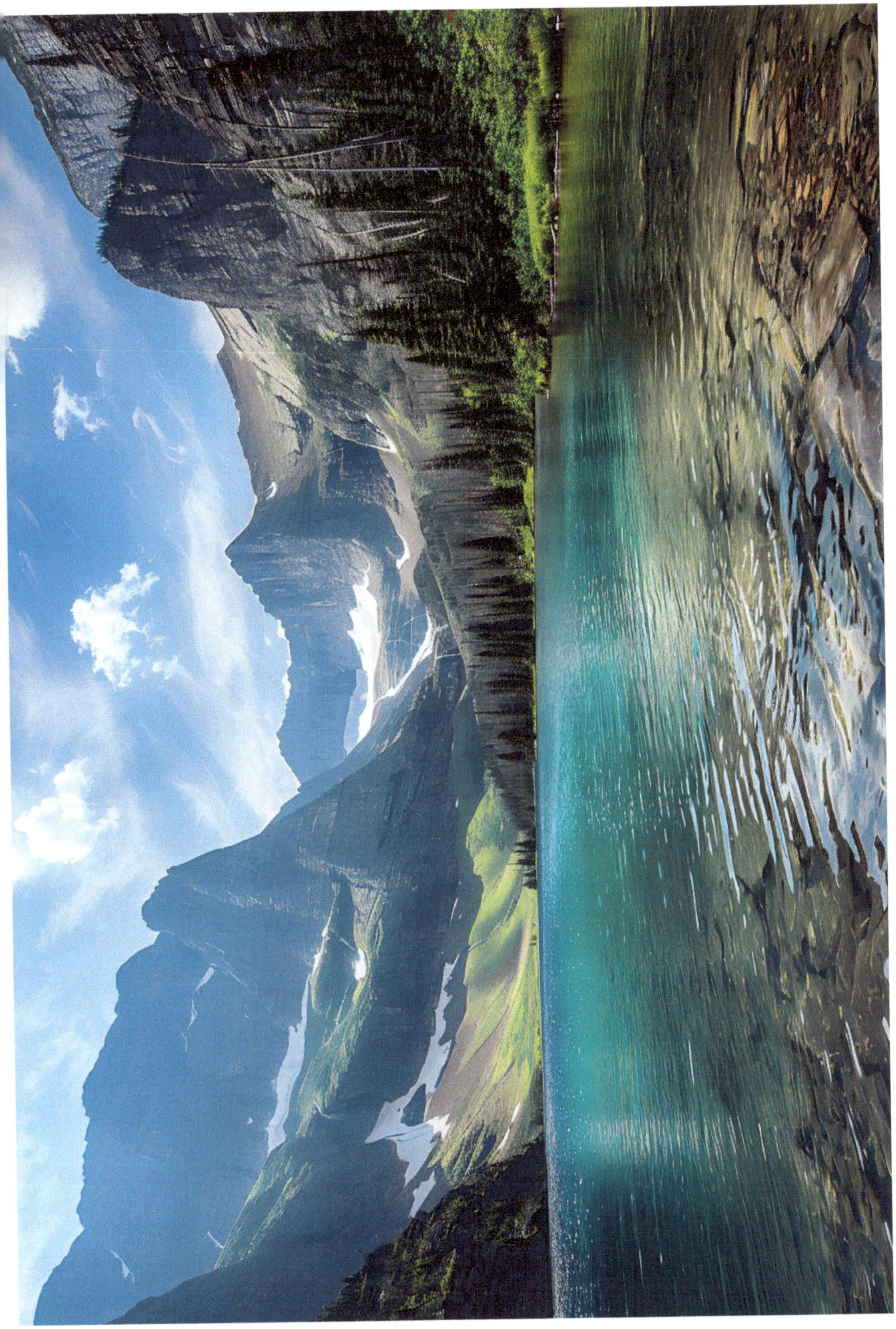

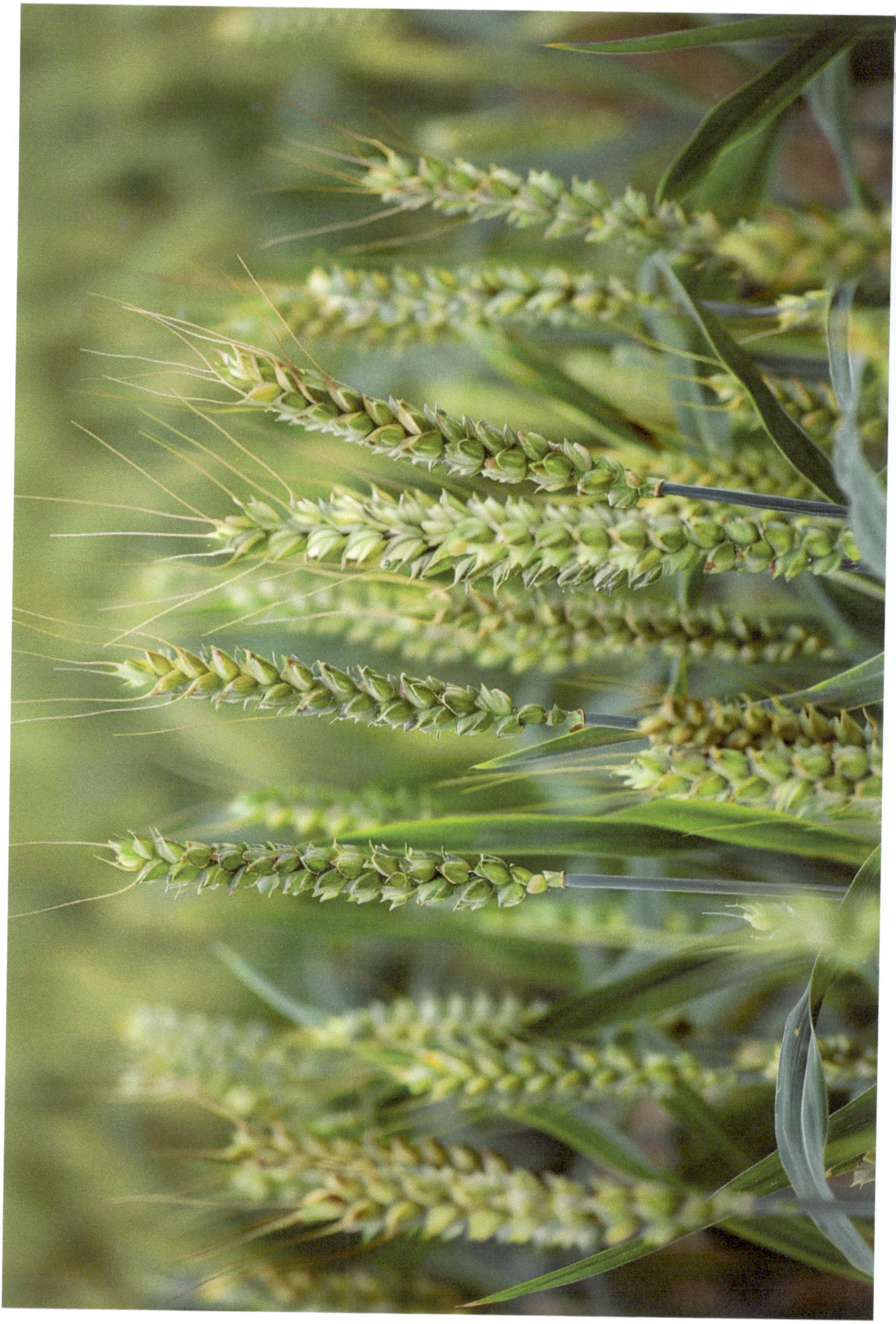

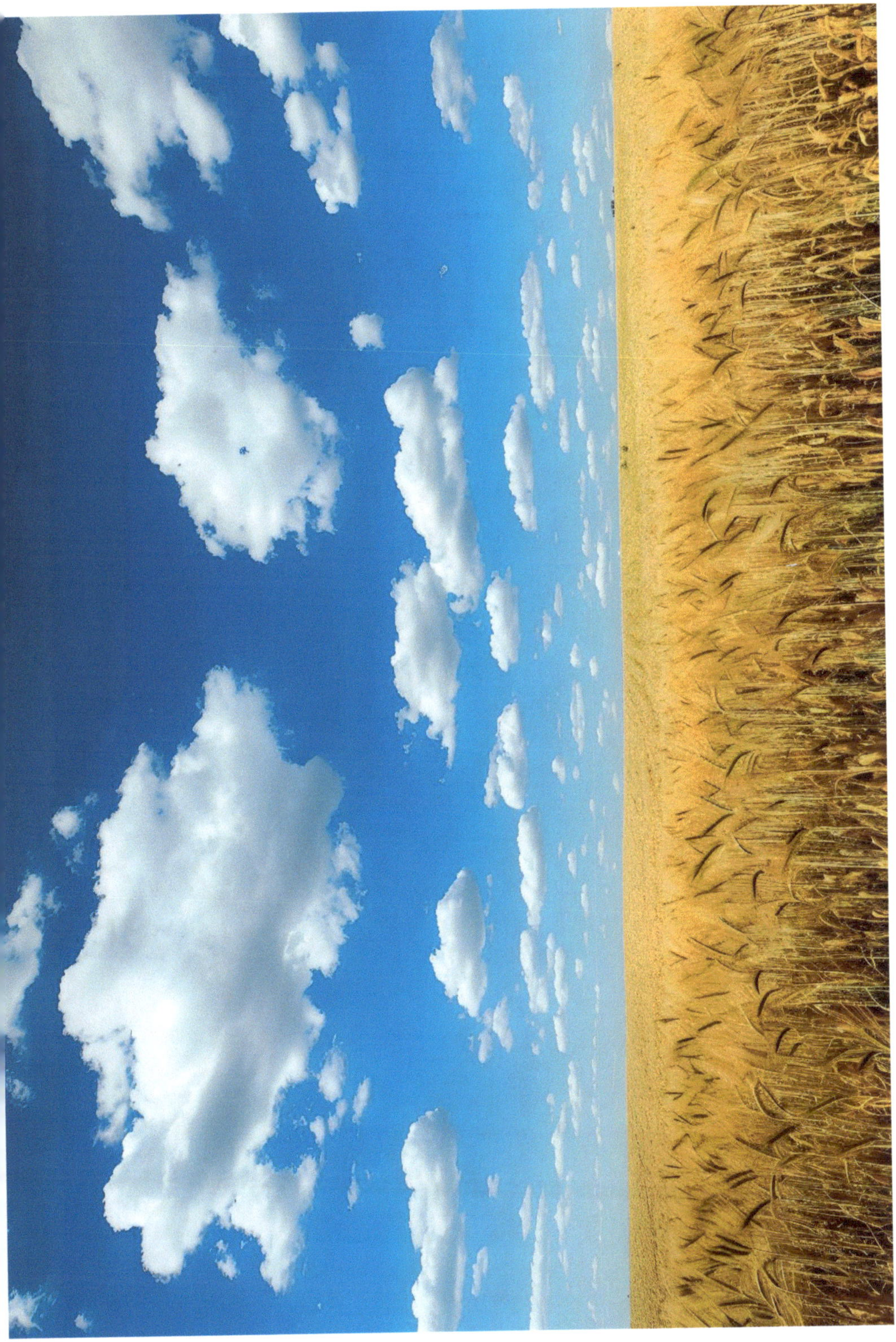

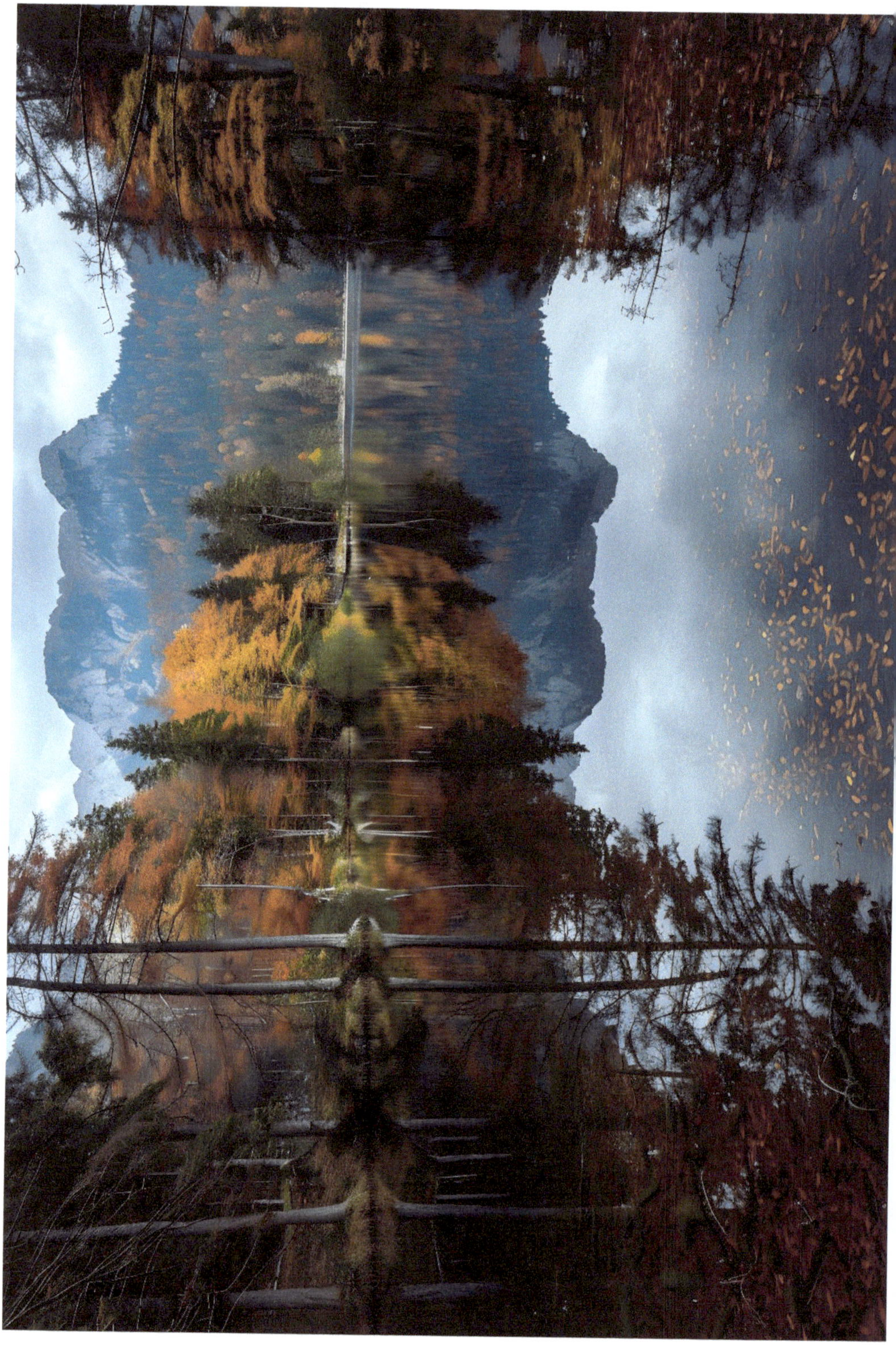

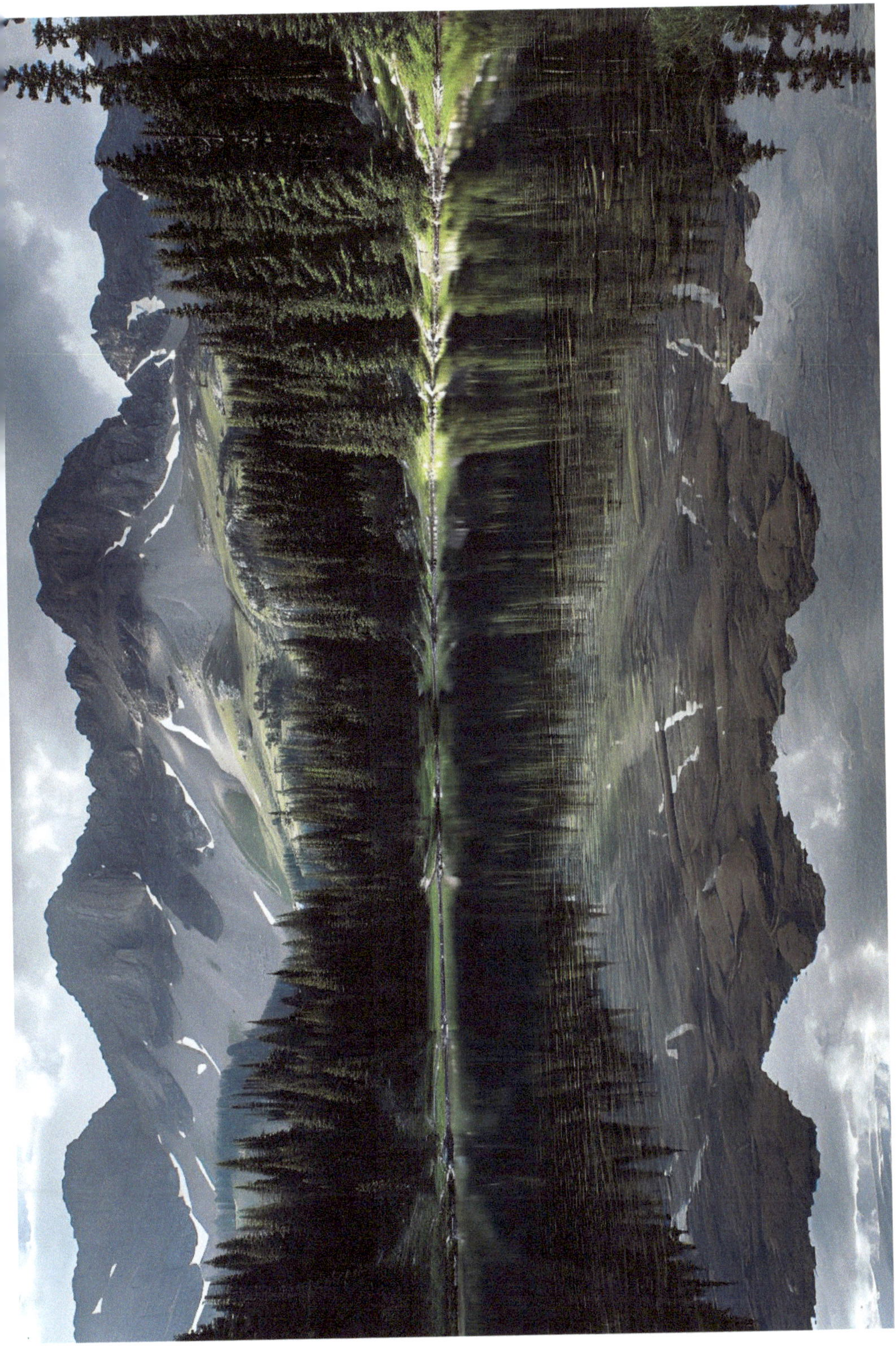

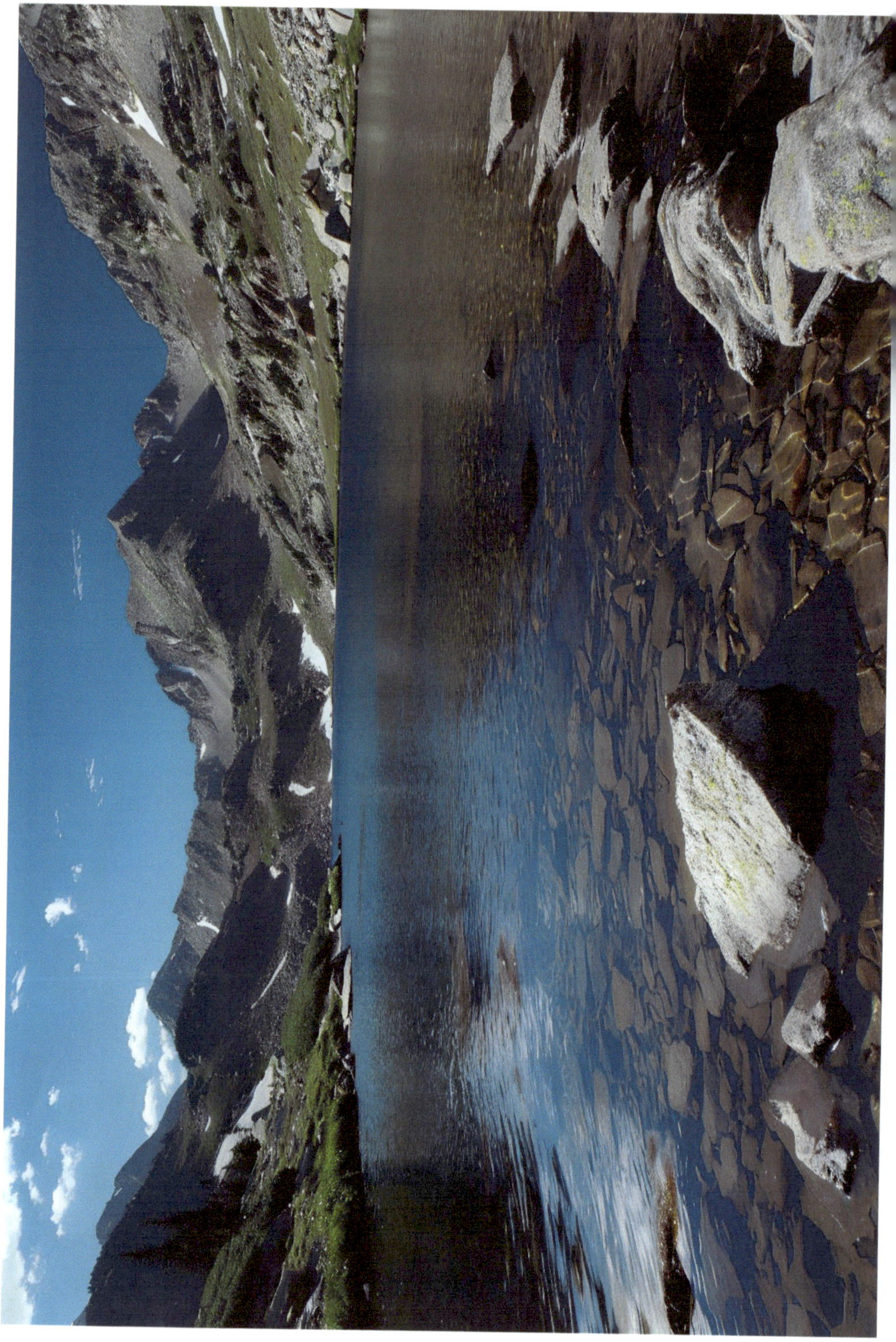

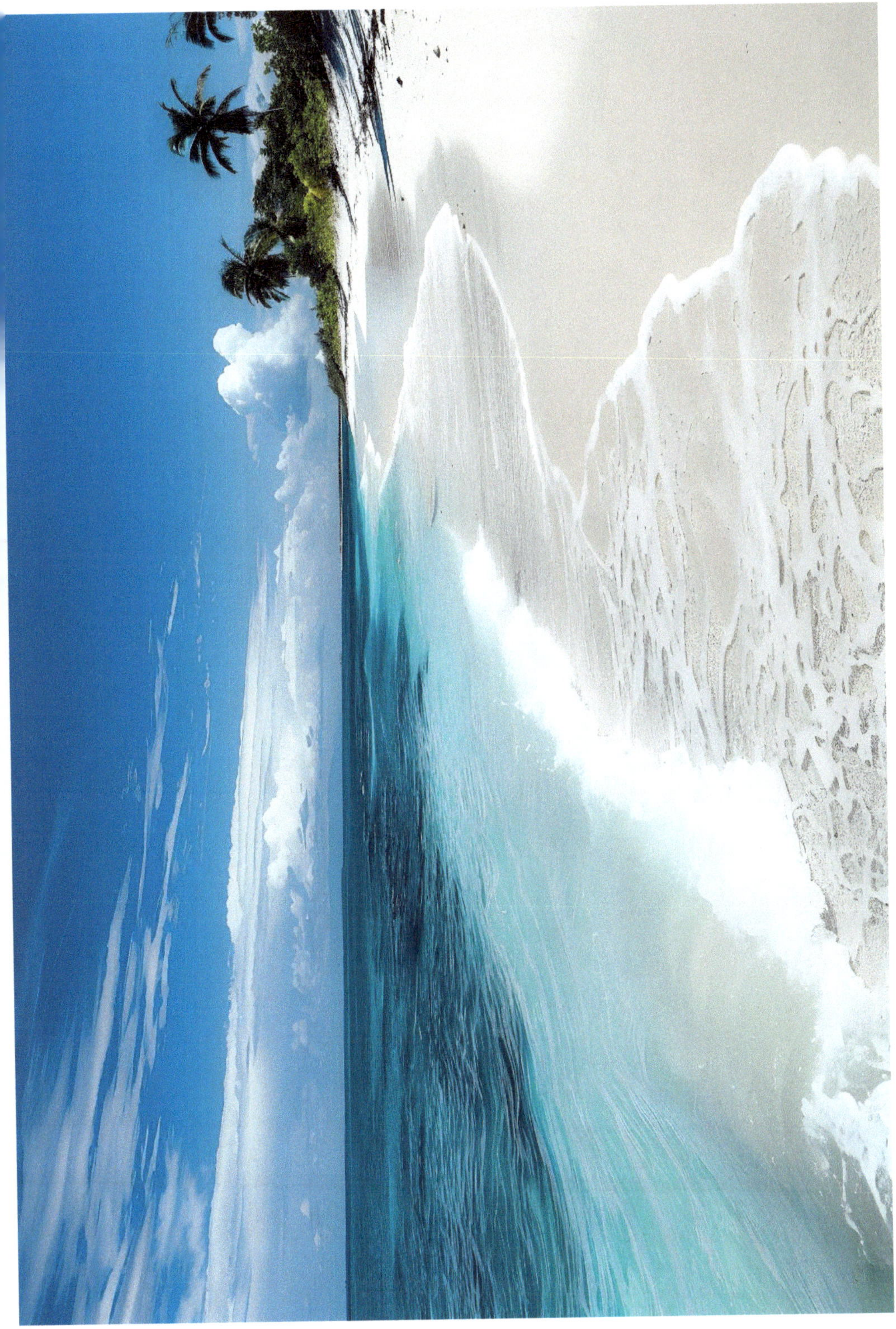

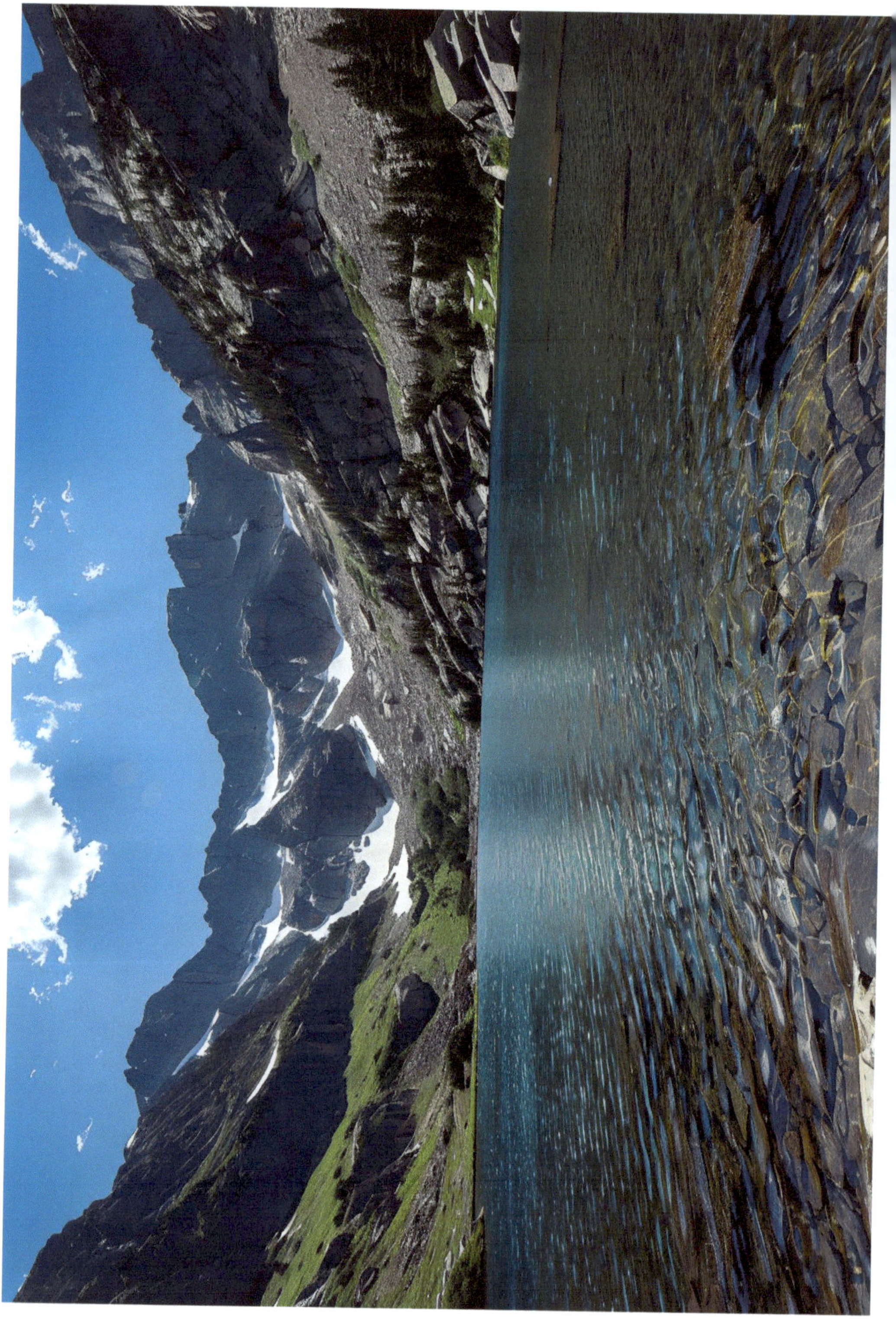

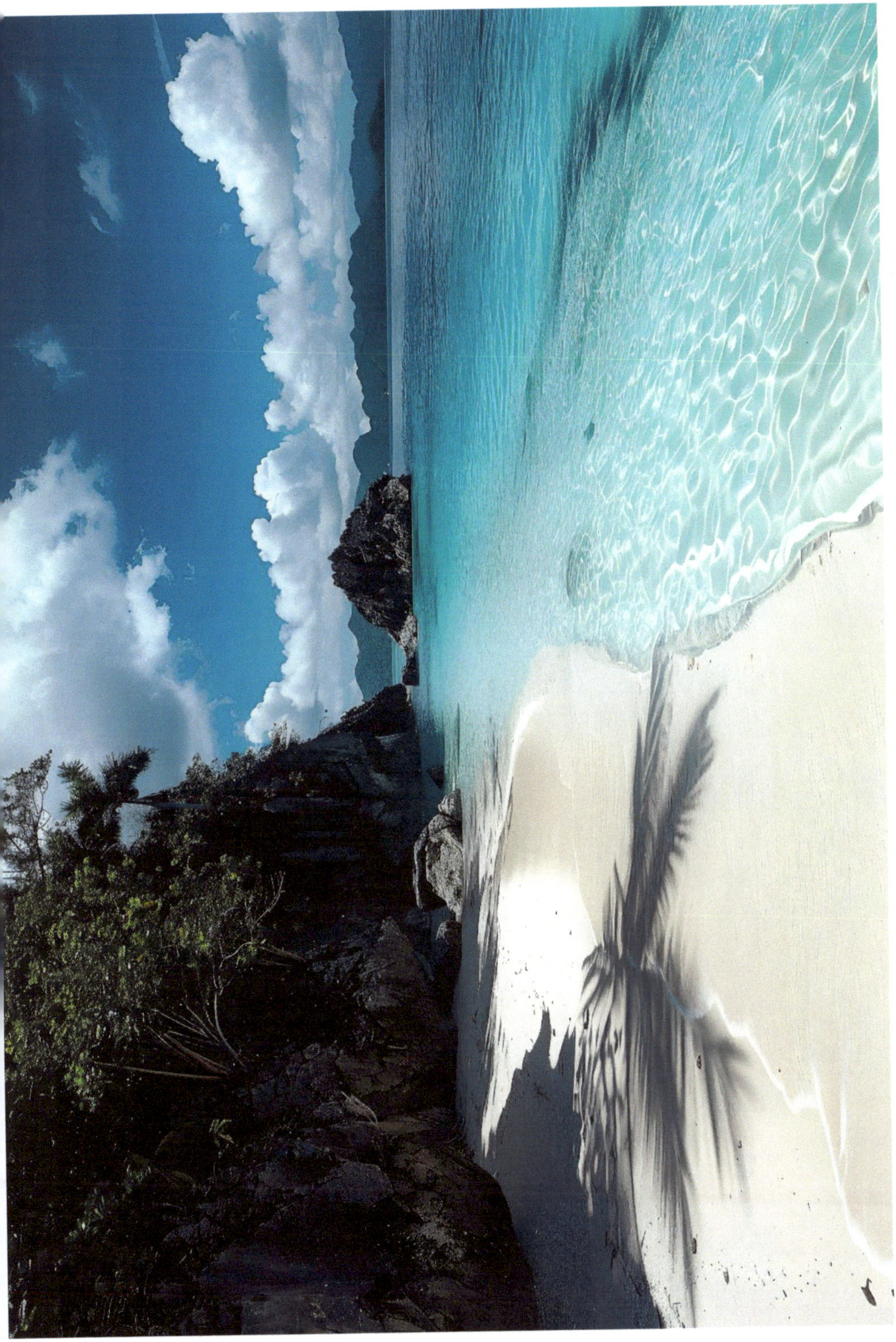

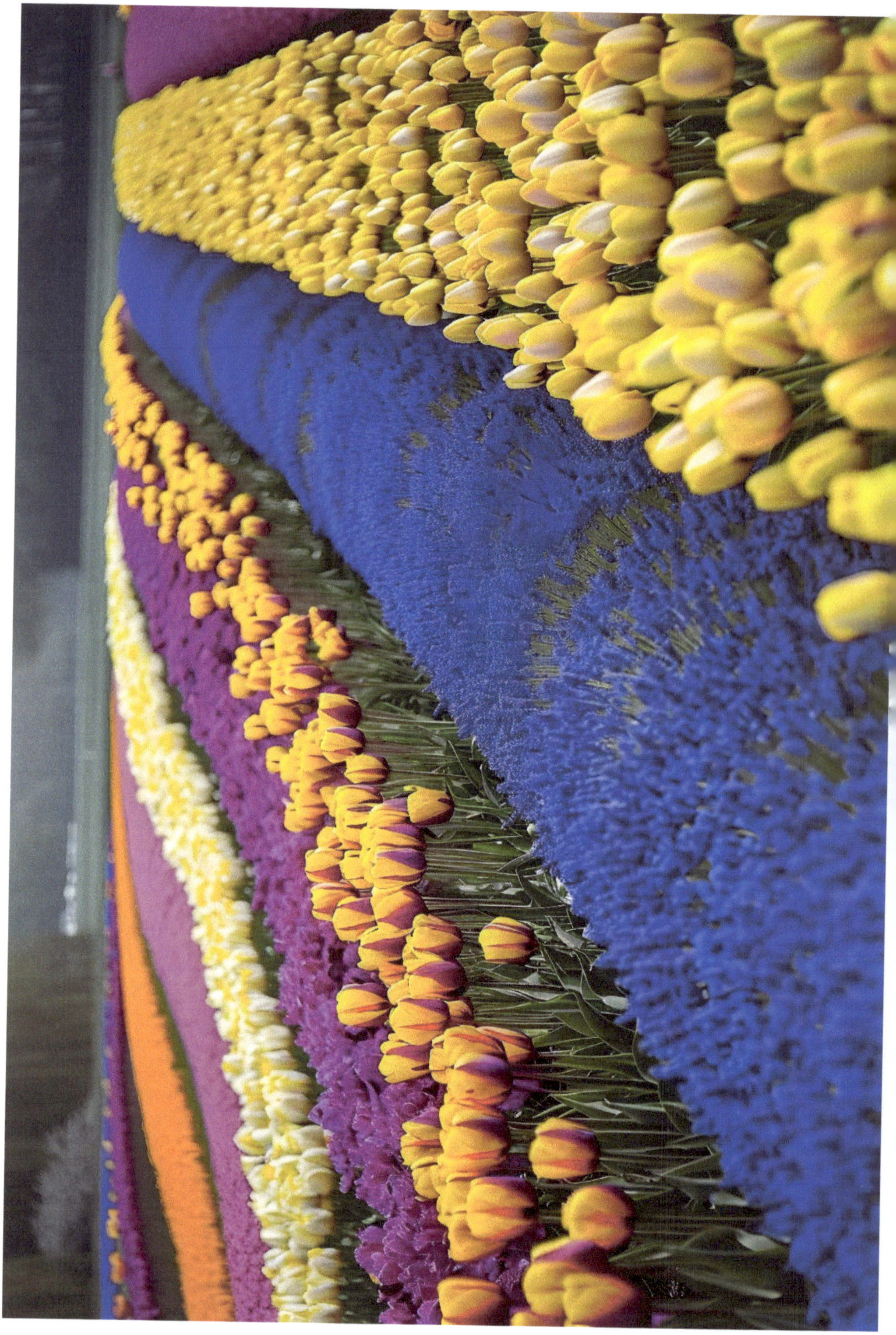

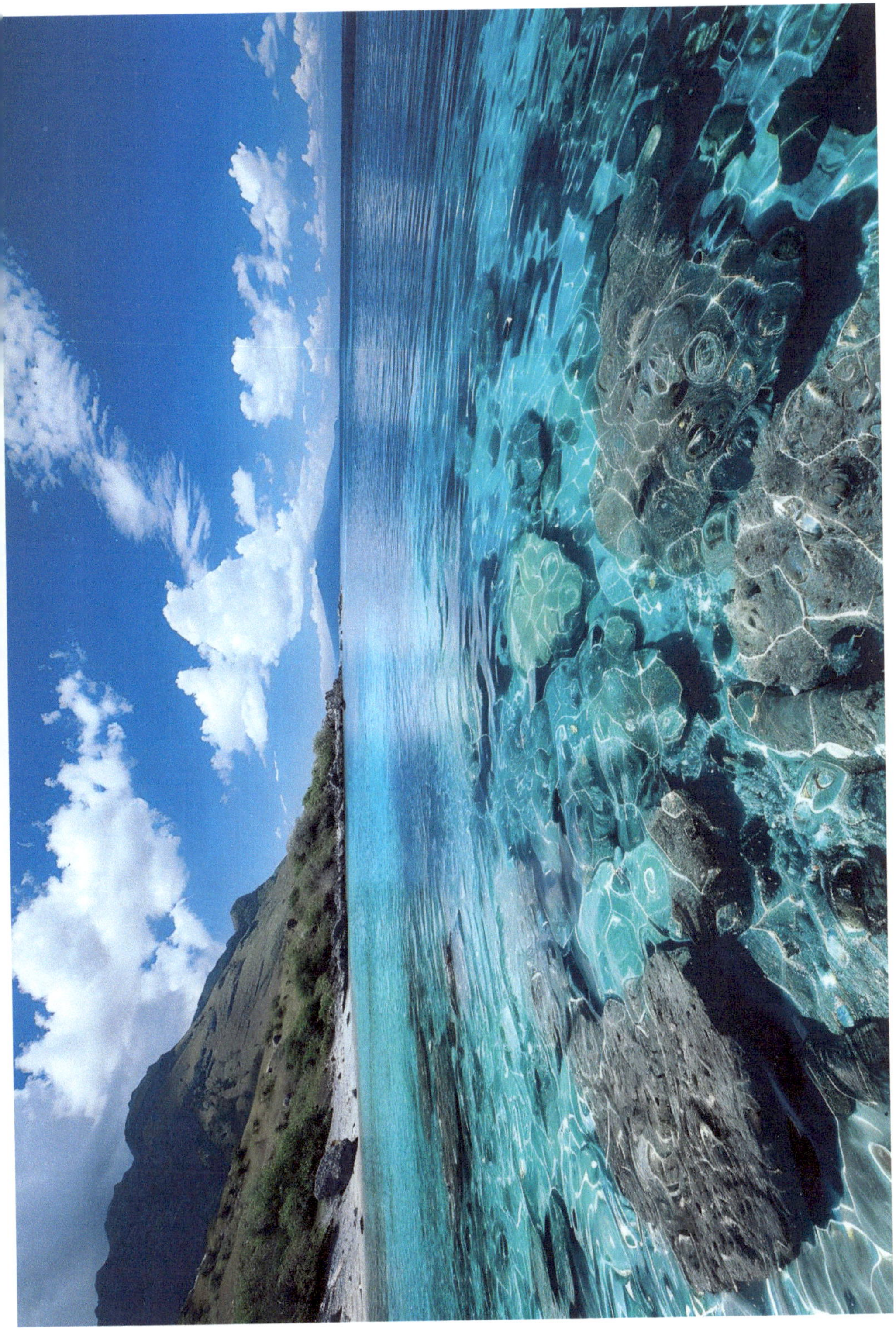

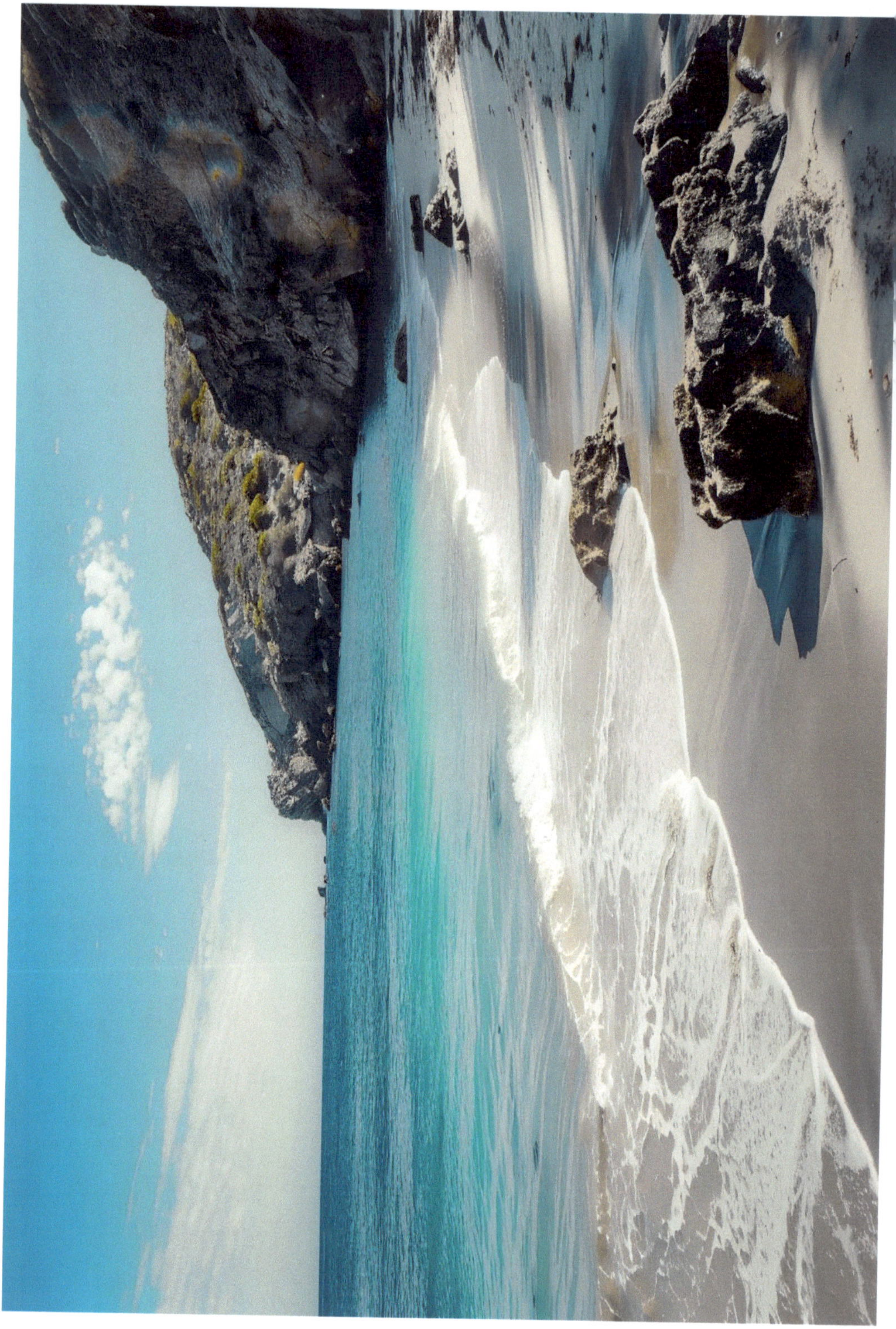

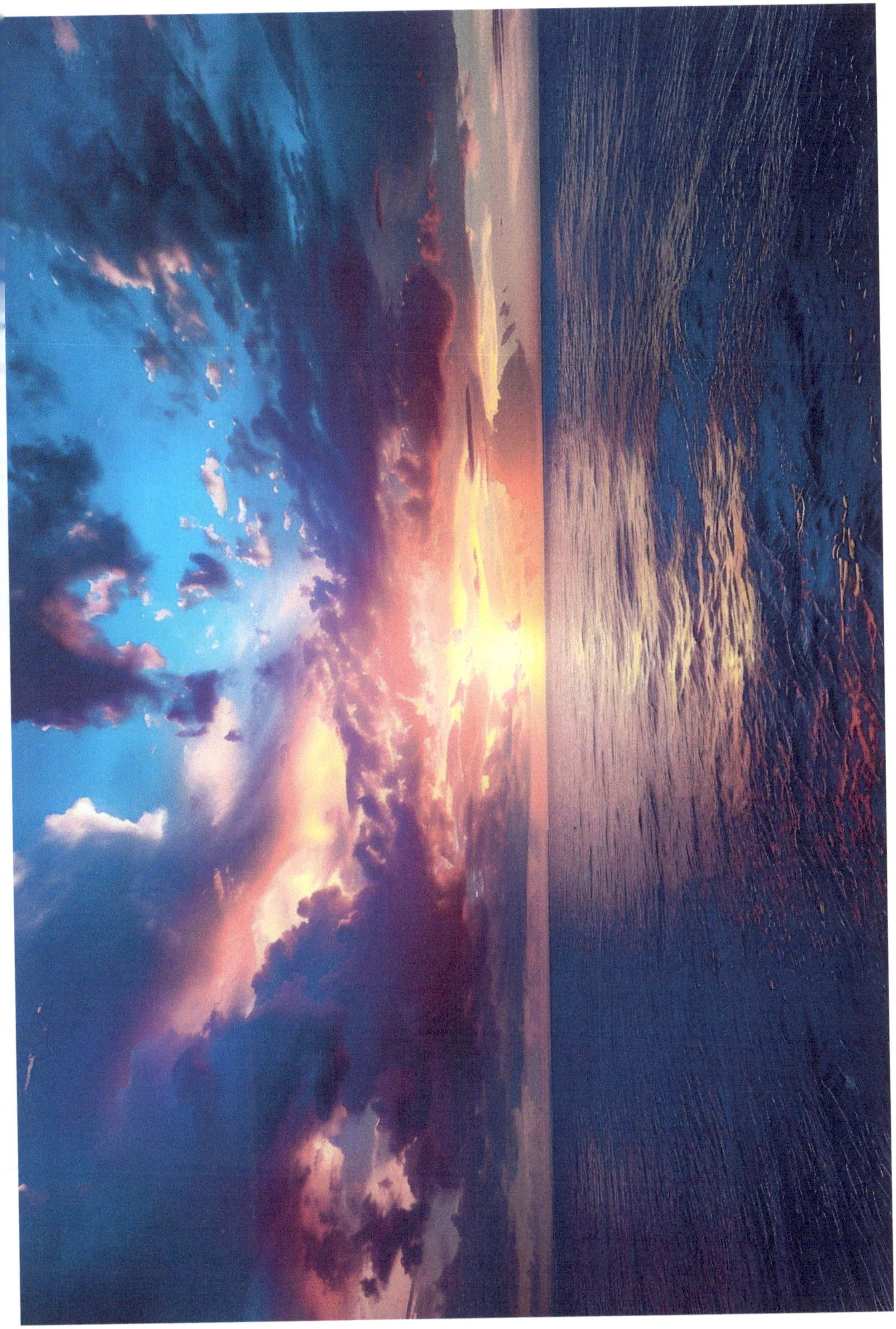

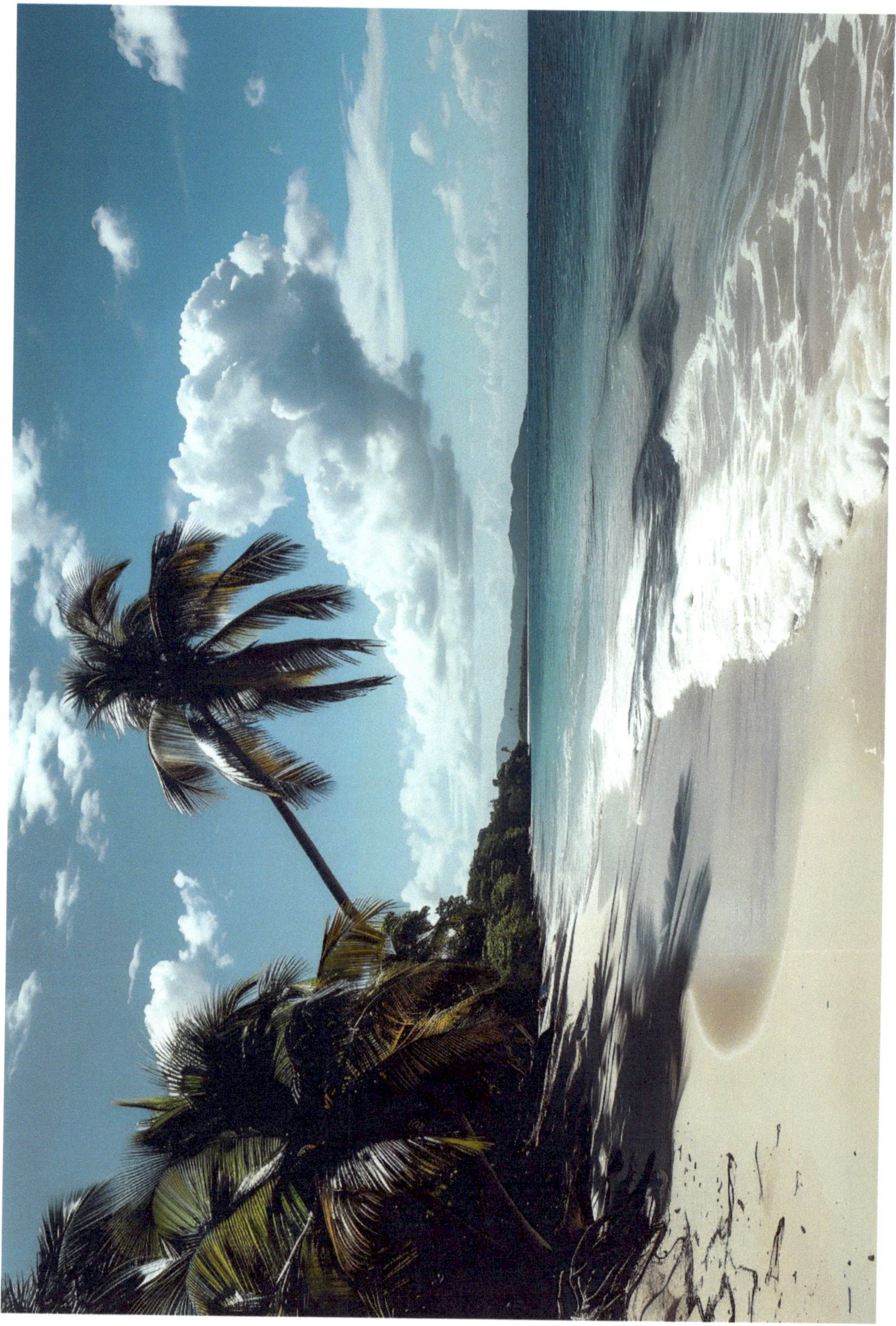